ANN OF AVA

ANN
OF AVA

BY

ETHEL DANIELS HUBBARD

Illustrated by
Margaret Ayer

Ayer Company Publishers, Inc.

ISBN 0-8369-8084-0 HARD COVER EDITION

ISBN 0-88143-166-4 PAPERBACK

LIBRARY OF CONGRESS CATALOG CARD NUMBER:

76-160921

PRINTED IN THE UNITED STATES

Contents

ANN OF AVA

Chapter 1

NANCY HASSELTINE

NANCY HASSELTINE came in from her favorite walk by the river and threw herself down in the big chair by the front window. It was April, and the air was intoxicatingly sweet with sunlight and the fragrance of the damp earth. Moreover, the river was riotously blue and turbulent, true to its Indian name, Merrimac, "the place of strong currents."

Nancy's cheeks flamed with color, her brown eyes shone with the fire of spring, and her curly hair was blown bewitchingly about her face. There was not a prettier girl in Bradford nor in all the valley of the Merrimac than Ann, generally known as Nancy, Hasseltine, and none more popular.

There seemed to be no limit to her love of good times and to her merry, laughing mood. She could bribe the bell-ringer at the academy with a smile. At home she was the life of the household. This last winter had been the gayest of all her sixteen years, thanks to that same little unpainted academy down the road, where more than eighty boys and girls were gathered in school.

There were no high schools in Nancy's day and no regular sessions of grammar or primary school. A small red school-house stood across the way from the meetinghouse, down near the frog pond and the alder swamp. Sometimes the men of the town would meet and vote to supply wood for the school fire during one or two months. Then school would keep, and the boys and girls would have a brief chance at book-learning.

By and by, in the spring of 1803, some wise parents decided that something must be done for the further education of their children. Whereupon about thirty of the "inhabitants of the First Parish in Bradford" — so the records read — met together and agreed to erect a building for an academy! They subscribed for shares in the building fund until fifteen hundred dollars was pledged. John Hasseltine, Nancy's father, gave a hundred dollars.

Then these enterprising New England settlers went to work and built the academy, completing it in just three months from the time of the meeting in March. Early in June the first term opened, at the time of year when schools nowadays are getting ready to close.

More than fifty pupils hastened to the new academy from Bradford and other Massachusetts towns, from Vermont, New Hampshire, and even from South Carolina, many of them traveling a long distance by stagecoach. Nancy Hasseltine and her three sisters were among the first pupils.

On the outside the building looked like a small district schoolhouse, such as we sometimes see today in the heart of the country. Inside were two classrooms, one on the right for the boys, another on the left for the girls. A narrow corridor separated them and projected somewhat in front. Above this projection a square tower rose to the height of a second story, culminating in an arched belfry in which hung the bell. Of course there was no dormitory, large or small, to house the pupils from far away, so they boarded around at the various farms.

The Hasseltine house, a few rods west of the academy on the "Boston Road," was the favorite resort of the boys and girls. Mr. Hasseltine was so heartily in sympathy with the young people that when he built his house he finished a hall at the rear of the second story to be used for their parties and entertainments.

After the new academy was opened, Nancy's hours outside school were packed full of merrymaking. This last winter there had been parties galore. The little village of Bradford, deviating from the prim traditions of New England, was a center of social gaiety.

Do not think that studies were seriously neglected, because, from the beginning, Bradford Academy stood for high standards, although in those early days the course of study was not so complex and difficult as it is thought to be in most schools today. The pupils acquired their knowledge of English grammar by reading and parsing the standard literature of the day, such as Pope's *Essay on Man* and

Paradise Lost. They made a fine art of penmanship, map drawing, and elaborate embroidery. Then, too, they studied English history, geography, arithmetic, and other subjects; and gradually the range of studies enlarged.

Fortunately for Nancy, she was as clever as she was beautiful, and lessons came as easily as fun-making. Moreover, with all her love of activity, she was devoted to reading. A good book could always beguile her into the cozy corner by the fireplace. Many lively discussions over their favorite authors were carried on among Nancy, her three sisters, and their mother, who was the greatest reader of them all. Yet in those festively gay months after Nancy's sixteenth birthday in December, studies and reading were pushed to the wall by a consuming interest in party dresses and party happenings. During that winter she outdid all her friends in frivolity, and none among them suspected the growing unrest in her soul.

With the coming of spring, however, the inner restlessness would no longer be hushed by gaiety. As the girl came indoors on that April afternoon, the pensive mood drew her irresistibly within its control. Her eyes grew big and dreamy with thought as she stretched her lithe figure comfortably in the armchair by the window, from which she looked out across the green fields to the river with its dark blue onrush of current.

Her three sisters, Abby and Mary and Rebecca, had not yet come in from the academy, and her father and mother were busy outdoors and in. Nancy was left alone with her thoughts there in the west room, which was deluged with the golden sunshine of late afternoon in springtime. In the evening there was to be a meeting in the upper parish, and she fought against her desire to go. Not for worlds would she have her schoolmates know that she had crept into a back seat at the meeting the other night and had suddenly found her face wet with tears. They should never suspect that something was tugging at her life deep down and making her most uncomfortable. She had been recklessly gay of late for the express purpose of covering up her real feelings. More than once her friends at school had predicted that something dreadful would happen to her unless she sobered down. In the "very heart of her soul" she *was* sobering down at a tremendous rate, though they did not surmise it.

As the girl gazed dreamy-eyed and wistful out toward the river, her mother lifted the latch of the door. Quickly Nancy sprang to her feet, so that her mother might not notice her unusual thoughtfulness. The old restlessness flashed back into her eyes and her easy bravado into her spirit and bearing. Mrs. Hasseltine looked searchingly at her youngest daughter, as she stood before her with flushed face and wind-tossed curls, her slight figure quivering with life. Her beauty was like that of the April day, all glow and color and promise.

Mrs. Hasseltine drew the girl into the warm, quiet kitchen where the sunlight and firelight mingled their gleam upon the low rafters. Together, mother and daughter prepared the evening meal. The teakettle swung on the crane humming its steamy song, the potatoes snapped in the ashes, and the smell of baked things came from the deep, brick oven.

As they worked, they talked and they thought, and sometimes their thoughts strayed far from their speech. Nancy was still struggling with those phantoms that haunted her mind and whose presence must be concealed. Her mother's heart was filled with hopes and fears for her youngest girl, who was so gay and sweet and impetuous, like the tumultuous river in springtime.

For Nancy the April days sped rapidly, and joy and song were in the air, even though a minor tune rang insistently in her heart.

One Sunday evening, Mr. Burnham, the principal of the academy, came to make a friendly call upon the Hasseltine family, as was his frequent habit. He was a young man, a Dartmouth student, who had taken charge of the school in Bradford the year before. There was something manly and earnest about him that won the respect and liking of his pupils and of people in general. This Sunday evening, with Mr. and Mrs. Hasseltine and the four girls, he talked in very straightforward fashion. Finally he made a remark that expressed Nancy's inner mood so exactly that she could hardly conceal her embarrassment. He said that sometimes people deliberately covered up their real feelings because they were afraid of becoming too serious. Nancy slipped out into the garden under the fruit trees to wrestle again with those troublesome thoughts that would not let her alone.

That night and for days after, she thought and thought until it seemed as if her brain would burst with thinking. She wondered if the Bible would help, but she could not understand the Bible very well. God seemed very far off and unapproachable. What should she do? She was too unhappy to pretend gaiety any longer, though not "for the whole world," as she wrote in her diary, would she have her school-mates know that she was disturbed by thoughts about God.

Frequently she shut herself in her room to read the books Mr. Burnham had given her and to try to pray. God still seemed remote and stern to the troubled mind of the girl, but gradually she began to realize that Jesus Christ was real and human and lovable. He could understand her per-fectly, and there was no fear in trusting her life to One who really knew and loved without limit. All the hero-worship of her soul went out to him in a great wave of loyalty. His perfect friendliness revealed God in a new light of infinite love and gentleness. The heavy weight of unhappiness that had dragged upon her spirits for so many weeks was fully and finally lifted.

Nancy was sixteen when she became a Christian, and sixteen also when with others of her school friends she joined the little church at Bradford. About the same time her father and mother became church members.

It was through Nancy, his favorite daughter, that John Hasseltine acknowledged himself a Christian. One summer evening the girl had knelt in her open window and the tears came as they often did in those days. Her father was crossing the field toward the house when he looked up and saw Nancy in all her loveliness kneeling and weeping. She was his idol, and as he looked at her he said to himself, "If my child, so sweet and innocent, weeps when she comes to God in prayer, what will become of me?" Whereupon he walked out on his farm, threw himself down under an oak tree and prayed. From that night he was willing to be known as a Christian man.

During the lovely summer days of the year 1806, when school was still in session, nearly all the boys and girls in Bradford Academy thought hard about serious things. As a result, many of them became Christians. The young principal, Mr. Burnham, was an inspiration to them all. For a time, classes were actually suspended so that teacher and pupils might talk and pray together and consider diligently what each might do to help bring the world to Jesus Christ.

During those same midsummer days, another group of students in another New England town were facing the same tremendous question and facing it with even greater definiteness of purpose. Through the "divinity that shapes our ends," those forces at work simultaneously at Bradford Academy and Williams College were to blend some day into one great student movement to reach around the world.

Among those whose lives were touched by the wonderful influence of Bradford Academy in those early days was a slender, flower-like girl named Harriet Atwood. She was one of the younger girls who had come the year before, when twelve years old, from her home across the river in Haverhill. In the sweet, sunshiny afternoons of July and August, Harriet and Nancy joined their schoolmates in lazy strolls down the grassy path that led from the academy into the depths of the wood. Red berries, trailing vines, and deep-scented ferns grew in the shade of the forest trees.

Upon a mossy bank the boys and girls sat and talked, with all the golden enthusiasm of youth, of the years to come and of the exploits they would do when they were men and women grown. With her brown eyes sparkling and her voice quivering with eagerness, Nancy spoke of service and heroism. Little Harriet, large eyed and serious, was already dreaming of sacrifice. But the long summer days and the "heart of the ancient wood" brought no revealing hint of those thrilling experiences that were to come within a few years into the lives of Harriet Atwood and Nancy Hasseltine.

Chapter 2

THE SHADOW OF
COMING EVENTS

FOUR years passed, and summer days came again to the valley of the Merrimac. During the last week of June a strange excitement stirred the little village of Bradford, from the covered bridge over the river unto the farthest farm on the Boston Road. In many a house busy preparations were being made for dinner and supper parties of varying size. At noon and sunset time guests from near and far would gather in the hospitable homes of Bradford for the ample repasts for which New England has always been famous.

With all the bustle and activity, a new and thrilling interest occupied the minds of the people. In the low-raftered kitchens and out upon the green roadsides lively discussion was carried on among young and old alike.

The cause of this unwonted excitement could have been

traced to the little parish meetinghouse that stood at the junction of the two roads, across the way from the Kimball Tavern. It was so simple that no chimney nor steeple dignified its exterior, yet beneath its humble gable roof a great, historic event was even now being enacted. In the boxed pews sat the black-robed ministers from the churches of Massachusetts who had come to Bradford for three long June days of deliberation concerning the problems of the New England parish. On horseback, by chaise, and by stagecoach they had journeyed, these "church fathers," as they were respectfully called.

On the second day profound astonishment seemed to take possession of the twenty-eight clergymen in the pews and to lay hold also upon the townspeople who had gathered in the galleries around the three sides. The air was electric with interest. Down near the front sat four young men upon whom all eyes were fastened. They were young college men now in Andover Theological Seminary. Early that morning they had walked the ten miles to Bradford in order to present to the Massachusetts ministers a momentous proposition. Their written petition had just been laid upon the communion table, after having been read in the clear, deep voice of Adoniram Judson, the spokesman of the group. A responsive thrill stirred the people as the young man took his seat. It was a bold project he had advocated, seeming scarcely reasonable, yet the conviction of the four students was contagious.

In the summer of 1806 this bold project had first crystallized into a serious purpose. Almost simultaneously with the religious awakening at Bradford Academy, five Christian students in Williams College had framed a far-reaching resolution. One hot day in August they went, according to habit, into a maple grove to pray together. The sky blackened with the approach of a thundershower, and they hastened to a near-by haystack for protection. There in the storm they talked about the vast old continent of Asia, concerning which they had read and studied. They told tales of the ignorance and wretchedness of its people, whereupon Samuel Mills for the first time unfolded his daring scheme of sending missionaries to those heathen lands, perhaps even offering their own lives for the great service. He grew more and more enthusiastic as he talked, until finally he exclaimed with a vehemence none of them ever forgot, "We can do it if we will!" Under his leadership a secret society called the Brethren was organized in Williams College, and those initiated united in the purpose to go themselves as missionaries to the non-Christian world.

After graduation, some of the Brethren, including Samuel Mills, went to Andover Seminary to study for the ministry. There they found kindred spirits in Samuel Newell from Union College, Samuel Nott from Harvard, and Adoniram Judson from Brown University, all of whom joined the order of the Brethren.

Everywhere he went Adoniram Judson became a recognized leader. He was brilliant, forceful, imaginative, and an indomitable worker. At Brown he had led his class, and at Andover he had received an offer dazzling to the ambition of a young theologian. He had been invited to become associate pastor of the largest church in Boston and in all New England as well. But his aspiration reached far beyond Boston and the bounds of his country, even to the ancient East, where no missionary from America had yet been sent. There he would go, and to a people who had never heard the name of Christ he would proclaim the Master whom he was learning to serve with passionate loyalty.

In the Bradford meetinghouse this June day in 1810, Adoniram Judson with the three "Samuels," his companions, boldly asked to be sent by the churches of Massachusetts *on a mission to the heathen world!* Never yet had a missionary gone from America to those countries beyond the seas, months and months away. American sailors who had touched the coasts of India, Burma, and Africa brought home tales of the awful degradation and savagery of the inhabitants. Most people thought it was an insane notion to dream of converting them to the Christian religion.

Conflicting ideas battled in the minds of the ministers. Upon first, and even second, thought the undertaking sounded wild and romantic; yet upon the faces of the young men they read clear-eyed conviction. They were confident that the voice of God had spoken. "We would better not try to stop God," said one of the ministers.

The assembly waited, hushed and uncertain, listening intently, as each of the young men told why he believed it his duty to give up home and friends and go on the long, perilous journey to the heathen world. As in modern business meetings, decision was referred to a committee of three who were to report on the morrow.

On Friday, the twenty-ninth of June, the committee appeared before the council and announced their verdict. They recommended that the purpose of the young men be approved, and, furthermore, that a foreign missionary board be organized in America to insure the support of the young volunteers and those who should follow their example. They even suggested its name, a long unwieldy one, the American Board of Commissioners for Foreign Missions.

Without a protest the report was adopted. It was a breathless moment for the four young men, who had hardly dared to dream such a victory possible. Every one present recognized that it was their tremendous earnestness that had won the day.

The session was dismissed for noon intermission. A group of ministers, Adoniram Judson in their midst, strolled up the road past the academy to Deacon Hasseltine's house, where they were invited to dine. In the west room the table had been laid for the noon dinner party. The Hasseltines had a widespread reputation for hospitality, which the tempting array of pies and cakes and other eatables amply justified.

To Nancy, the youngest daughter of the household, fell the task of serving her father's guests. As she watched them coming up the path from the gate, her flashing eyes revealed her interest in the day's unusual event.

At twenty she was even more beautiful than she had been at sixteen, for a sweet thoughtfulness tempered the old laughing gaiety of eyes and mouth. Her cheeks were flushed

with the heat and excitement of the day; her soft curls clustered about her fair neck. Of all the varied beauty of the day in June nothing was so wondrous fair as the girl Nancy.

As the guests entered the room a pair of keen, fearless brown eyes met hers, and their gaze lingered as if spell-bound. From the moment Adoniram Judson and Nancy Hasseltine looked into each other's eyes a great and wonderful experience was born in the lives of both.

During the meal, Adoniram Judson, noted for his ready wit and social grace, was unaccountably silent. For some reason he seemed strangely preoccupied with his plate. Nancy, who had heard of his eloquent speech, his daring proclamation of his beliefs, marveled at his stubborn silence. As she cut the pies on the broad window sill she cast a furtive glance at the young man who was the hero of the hour, but who could not be persuaded to talk. Little did she dream that his thoughts were forcibly diverted from the absorbing theme that his companions still discussed, and that deep down in his mind he was composing a sonnet in honor of the loveliest girl he had ever seen.

Chapter 3

GIRL PIONEERS

ONE day, about a month after the eventful gathering in the meetinghouse, the Boston stagecoach brought to Bradford a certain small piece of mail destined to become of large importance in the lives of two people. It was a letter carefully sealed with wax and in fine, firm handwriting, addressed to Miss Nancy Hasseltine. As the girl broke the seal, joy and fear mingled for one fleeting instant upon her face.

For many days the letter lay unanswered, but Nancy went about the house and along the grassy highways of Bradford with the light of a great wonder shining in her eyes. Persistently, however, she feigned indifference and deliberately postponed reply to the letter.

Finally, her sister, exasperated by her procrastination, said to her, "Have you answered that letter of Mr. Judson's?"

"No," retorted Nancy with a toss of her brown curls.

"Then if you don't, I shall," responded the older sister.

The threat had the desired effect, and in course of time a letter written and sealed by Nancy Hasseltine reached Adoniram Judson at Phillips Hall, Andover. That letter brought an interesting challenge to the young man who all his life had pushed his way through every obstacle to the goal of his ambition. In her girlish perversity and in her real perplexity, Nancy had written a cool, discouraging reply to his eager letter. Adoniram Judson perceived her dilemma, for with his fine sense of honor he realized keenly the tremendous sacrifice he was demanding of the girl he loved in asking her to become his wife.

He might have offered her a comfortable home in the city of Boston as the wife of one of its leading clergymen. There her beauty and intelligence would have shone in conspicuous brightness. Instead, he was inviting her to share the uncertain lot of the first missionary from America to the mysterious regions of southern Asia. It was perfectly reasonable to expect suffering and privation, even persecution and death. Yet he believed Ann Hasseltine was capable of just that high heroism that such a life demanded. This glad belief drew his steps confidently toward Bradford during those wonderful summer days that were bringing deep heart-searchings to the young man and woman.

Nancy was struggling with a question that no woman in America had yet been called upon to face. Should she marry the man who was consuming her thoughts and go to a distant land, probably never to return?

"No," said nearly every one whose advice was sought, or who proffered an opinion unasked.

"It is altogether preposterous for a woman to consider such a rash undertaking."

"It is utterly improper," said one.

"It is wild and romantic," said another.

Mr. Kimball, the father of one of Nancy's school friends, declared that he would tie his daughter to the bedpost before he would let her go. But the girl Nancy, with her old independent spirit deepened by a new sense of duty, followed the call of God, regardless of unsympathetic comments.

There were a few people who stood by her and encouraged her to dare all and go. Among them was her sister Abigail, that tall, self-possessed girl who afterwards became principal of Bradford Academy and retained that position for forty years. Abby and Nancy were great chums, understanding each other easily, even though they were quite unlike in temperament, perhaps because of that very fact.

Abigail was teaching school in Beverly, and late in the summer her young sister went to visit her. While there Nancy wrote the following letter, in the rather ponderous English used in her time, to her old school friend, Lydia, who lived near her in Bradford:

Beverly, September 8, 1810

I have ever made you a confidant. I will still confide in you and beg for your prayers that I may be directed in regard to the subject which I shall communicate. I feel willing, and expect, if nothing in providence prevents, to spend my days in this world in heathen lands. Yes, Lydia, I have about come to the determination to give up all my comforts and enjoyments here, sacrifice my affection to relatives and friends, and go where God, in his providence, shall see fit to place me. My determinations are not hasty or formed without viewing the dangers, trials, and hardships attendant on a missionary life. Nor were my determinations formed in consequence of an attachment to an earthly object; but with a sense of my obligation to God, and with a full conviction of its being a call of providence, and consequently my duty. My feelings have been *exquisite* in regard to the subject. Now my mind is settled and composed, and is willing to leave the event with God — none can support one under trials and afflictions but he. In him alone I feel a disposition to confide.

There was another girl friend of the old academy days who must be told the great news of her engagement and missionary purpose. So, one October morning after her return to Bradford, Nancy went through the covered bridge that led across the Merrimac into Haverhill, up the hill to the town square and on to the house of Harriet Atwood. Harriet had just passed her seventeenth birthday, and Nancy would be twenty-one in December. To her little friend Nancy confided her expectation of becoming the wife of a missionary to India. Harriet's big, brown eyes grew misty with wonder and sympathy. In her diary that night she wrote these words in a style that resembled Nancy's:

How did this news affect my heart! Is she willing to do all this for God; and shall I refuse to lend my little aid in a land where divine revelation has shed its clearest rays? I have felt more for the salvation of the heathen this day than I recollect to have felt through my whole past life. . . . What can I do, that the light of the gospel may shine upon them? They are perishing for lack of knowledge, while I enjoy the glorious privileges of a Christian land. Great God, direct me! Oh, make me in some way beneficial to their immortal souls!

In less than a month that same little diary of Harriet's bore this entry:

Sleep has fled from me and my soul is enveloped in a dark cloud of troubles! Oh that God would direct me; that he would plainly mark out the path of duty and let me not depart from it.

In that short interim, Samuel Newell, one of the missionary volunteers, had come into Harriet's life; and by night and by day the thoughts of the girl were dream-haunted.

The winter passed and the spring days came again. One April evening while Harriet was visiting her sister in Charlestown, she came back from Boston to find — a letter! Just a slip of paper with a few strokes of the pen upon it, but what agitation that can produce in a girl's inner being! She broke the seal and read the words and the name she had expected, yes, dreaded to see. To Harriet, as to Nancy, had come the great testing of love and loyalty.

Through the tears that dimmed her eyes Harriet wrote a few days later in her diary:

The important decision is not yet made. I am still wavering. I long to see and converse with my dear mother! So delicate is my situation that I dare not unbosom my heart to a single person. What shall I do? Could tears direct me in the path of duty, surely I should be directed — My heart aches: — I know not what to do! — "Guide me, O thou great Jehovah." I shall go home on

Tuesday. Perhaps my dear mother will immediately say: *Harriet shall never go*. Well, if this should be the case my duty would be plain. I cannot act contrary to the advice and express commands of a pious mother.

When Tuesday came, Harriet mounted the stagecoach that traveled between Boston and Haverhill and came again to her mother's house in the town square. Before crossing the Merrimac the stage lumbered through Bradford along the Boston Road, past the academy and the Hasseltine house. The youngest and fairest daughter of that Bradford household and the slender, brown-eyed girl of Haverhill were destined not many months hence to leave the sunny farms of New England, even the dear home people around the family hearth and go out across two oceans to the mysterious land of southern Asia and spend their lives among its pagan people.

Harriet found her mother already prepared for the solemn question that was invading their home. In his stress of mind, Samuel Newell had made a confidant of Nancy Hasseltine, and she had been the bearer of his troubled request to Harriet's mother. With tears in her eyes, that loyal Christian woman replied, "I dare not, I cannot speak against it." Thus, when Harriet came home that April day, Mrs. Atwood was ready to trust the great decision to her daughter's conscience.

Since her father's death, three years before, Harriet had clung with increasing affection to her mother. Now, a wonderful, new love was surging up in her life, transforming her from a girl into a woman and supplying her with irresistible purpose. Samuel Newell had drawn out the deepest love of her maiden heart. Yet not alone for the sake of her lover did she decide upon the difficult life of a missionary, but because she was determined down to the depths of her pure soul to go wherever God should lead her.

In June, Harriet and Samuel were compelled to part for nine long months, as the young man was going to Philadelphia to join his friend Gordon Hall in the study of physics and medicine by way of further preparation for their missionary work. It was a lonely heart that was left behind in the house in Haverhill. Nancy Hasseltine would have been a great comfort, but Nancy was away on a long visit in Salem.

Early in the winter Nancy had said good-by to Adoniram Judson as he had set forth on a far longer journey than the stage route to Philadelphia. He had sailed on the ship *Packet* for England, having been sent to London by the directors of the new American missionary society to confer with the older English society as to some possible combination between the two organizations.

In those days a voyage to Europe was a snail-like process consuming two months of time. Letters traveled even more slowly, so that Adoniram Judson could well-nigh come again to the valley of the Merrimac before Nancy would hear of his arrival on the English shore. Hence it was many weeks before the news reached Bradford of the exciting adventures that befell the young man on his trip across the Atlantic.

His ship was captured by a French privateer and he was

taken prisoner to Bayonne, France. For six weeks he was detained there, although early in his captivity he had been released from prison on parole and allowed to board with an American family in the city.

It was the sixth of May before he reached London, and in June, his business completed, he sailed on the ship *Augustus* for New York. The last of August brought him to his father's home in Plymouth and to that other home on the banks of the river in Bradford.

The return of Adoniram Judson with his message from England was the signal for another meeting of the men who had gathered in the Bradford church a year and more ago. On the eighteenth of September, the church fathers, now the officers and members of the new missionary society, assembled in the town of Worcester, Massachusetts.

Adoniram Judson, slight of build, even boyish in appearance, but with piercingly bright eyes and resonant voice, stood forth and announced his decision. A joint missionary enterprise between England and America had been disapproved by the leaders in London, but the London Missionary Society was willing to adopt the American volunteers as its missionaries and promptly send them forth to their distant posts of service. Consequently — and here Adoniram Judson exhibited his tremendous power of determination — if the American society refused his appointment, he would become a missionary of the English organization. Samuel Nott announced a similar resolve.

The unyielding purpose of the young men proved the needed spur to action, and the American Board of Commissioners for Foreign Missions then and there appointed its first missionaries, Adoniram Judson, Samuel Newell, Samuel Nott, and Gordon Hall. For a second time victory was scored by means of the bold consecration of the missionary volunteers.

The autumn days deepened into winter, and hope and dread stirred the lives of Nancy and Harriet, Adoniram and Samuel. The time of their departure was drawing near.

In January an exciting message came from Samuel Newell and Gordon Hall in Philadelphia. In two weeks the ship *Harmony* was to sail from that city to Calcutta, and the government would permit missionaries to take passage. A second war with England was threatening, and if they did not sail at once, ports might be blockaded and departure long deferred.

Should they go? It was a terrific question that pressed for immediate answer upon the officers of the young mission board. Only a small sum of money was in the treasury, not enough to pay the passage fees. Was it reasonable to expect that the actual departure of missionaries for a heathen country would attract attention and awaken sympathy to such an extent that gifts of money would be forthcoming? Should they boldly venture and bravely trust? Long and anxiously they prayed and deliberated, seeking to discern the right. At last the vote was cast, and the verdict was — *the missionaries shall go!*

To the Hasseltine and Atwood homes came the word that Nancy and Harriet must soon take their marriage vows and say farewell, perhaps forever, to their childhood homes.

The piercing winds of a New England winter swept through the valley of the Merrimac and along the snowy highways of Bradford, when, on the fifth of February, a group of people gathered in the west room of the Hasseltine house. A strange hush fell upon the little company, and tears were close to the eyes of every guest.

Harriet Atwood sat by the side of Samuel Newell, her betrothed, a sad seriousness resting upon her. But the center of interest was the radiant, beautiful face of Nancy Hasseltine as she gave her hand and heart in marriage to the missionary, Adoniram Judson, whom, less than two years before, she had first met in this very room. Her brave, unfaltering eyes shone with a wonderful light as Pastor Allen gave the two young people his blessing, called them his dear children, and spoke lovingly of the labors they were to perform.

From that night the girl Nancy, popular, clever, beautiful, became the woman resourceful and heroic, who was destined to be known in three continents as Ann Hasseltine Judson, the heroine of Ava.

Chapter 4

A LONG GOOD-BY

ALTHOUGH it was a bitterly cold day in February the streets of Salem were well filled with people. Involuntarily on such a day one would hover near the cheery kitchen fireplace with its savory warmth. Instead, the people of this seacoast town seemed to be drawn forth, as by the spell of a Hamelin piper, toward one enchanted spot, the white meetinghouse known as Tabernacle Church.

From neighboring towns sleighs brought bundled, shivering folk along the snowy roads to Salem. From Andover, a delegation of students, boys and young men, walked the entire sixteen miles in the freezing cold of early morning, returning on foot late in the afternoon. But cold and weariness were speedily forgotten in the great and absorbing interest that centered in the day's events in Tabernacle Church.

On this sixth day of February, 1812, five young men were

to be ordained as Christian ministers and commissioned by the church of America as its first missionaries to a heathen country. In imagination people pictured the separation from home, the long voyage across the gray, wintry ocean, and the possible hostility and persecution of the savage inhabitants of those distant regions. Every heart felt a throb of sympathy for those dauntless young people who had already left their homes and were soon to depart from their native land, perhaps forever.

Near the front of the church, before the distinguished clergymen from Boston, Salem, and other towns, knelt five volunteers for missionary service, Adoniram Judson, Samuel Newell, Samuel Nott, Gordon Hall, and a new recruit, Luther Rice. A hand of fatherly blessing was laid upon each youthful head bowed in willing consecration to God and obedience to his call.

Kneeling there before the elder ministers, these young men in their purity and earnestness resembled Sir Galahad as he knelt before his superior knight, Sir Launcelot, to receive the "high order of knighthood." For a more perilous quest than that of Sir Galahad for the Holy Grail, they vowed their allegiance as knights of the great King whose Round Table is in very truth the whole, round world.

During the dedication service many eyes turned from the young missionaries to linger lovingly upon a girlish figure kneeling reverently by the side of a boxed pew near the front. A scoop bonnet, the fashion of the day, covered her brown curls and partly shielded the brave, beautiful face of Mrs. Adoniram Judson, the bride of a single day.

On her long visit in Salem, Nancy Hasseltine had become well known in town. Moreover, in her school days, stories of her gaiety and beauty had drifted through the countryside — stories that reached a high climax in the announcement of her decision to go as a foreign missionary — an unprecedented career for an American woman. A solemn joy seemed to radiate through her kneeling figure during the service that sacredly sealed her marriage vows.

Another girlish face tugged hard at the heartstrings of the people. It was that of Harriet Atwood, the young woman who within a few days would become the bride of Samuel Newell and go with him across the great seas to a new home in the Far East. She was a fragile flower of girlhood, apparently unfitted for storm and tempest, but those who looked into the depths of her sad, brown eyes read there the indomitable purpose dwelling in her frail body.

At the close of that memorable day, Samuel Nott, Gordon Hall, and Luther Rice took their departure for Philadelphia, expecting to sail in a few days on the *Harmony* for Calcutta. The others lingered in Beverly and Salem, waiting for wind and tide to favor the sailing of the brig *Caravan* from the port of Salem bound for the coast of Asia.

Already the little boat was rocking at its moorings out in the harbor. Compared with the gigantic steamships that cross the ocean today, she was a baby craft of perhaps five hundred tons. On board, her crew were receiving freight and provisions for the long voyage around the Cape of Good Hope to India.

On shore, four persons looked anxiously each day out toward the black masts of the ship that was to bear them away from everything dear and familiar into experiences that God alone knew. Enough that he knew and would provide for the whole, uncertain future of their lives!

On Monday, the seventeenth of February, a terrific storm fell upon Salem, almost burying the town in snow. The next day dawned bleak and cold, with a presage in the air of coming events.

Before the forenoon was past the desired and dreaded summons became a reality. A message was brought to the Judsons and Newells requesting them to go on board at once, that the ship might be ready to sail with the first friendly breeze.

The inevitable "last things" were hastily collected and carried down to the wharf. The sleigh stood at the door and the long, long good-bys must be said. Down through the snowy streets of Salem to the end of the lowest wharf in town the missionaries were driven, thence to be transferred by the custom-house boat to the *Caravan* out in the bay.

It was a dreary, frigid day, but nevertheless a number of friends gathered at the end of the pier to show their sympathy with the young missionaries and their brave purpose. During the two weeks of waiting for the *Caravan* to sail, interest in the new undertaking had mightily deepened. Even those opposed could not check their hearts' impulse to lavish kindness upon the missionaries and their youthful brides. A purse of fifty dollars was left at the door one day with the label, "For Mr. Judson's private use." Best of all, money for outfits and salaries had been almost miraculously provided. On January twenty-seventh only twelve hundred dollars was in the treasury of the new mission board. Within three weeks more than six thousand dollars had been freely given, and by the time the two ships *Harmony* and *Caravan* sailed the needs of the missionaries were supplied for a year in advance.

The west wind, which throughout the day had given promise of departure to the long-delayed ship, died away at dusk and thus removed all hope of sailing that night. From the deck of the *Caravan* the surrounding scene was desolation itself. The sky overhead was ominously black and dark, and stormy waters stretched away seaward toward the far horizon.

On shore, dim little lights spoke tantalizingly of home. But within, the cabin of the Judsons presented a sharp contrast to the dolefulness without. Adoniram and Ann Judson, Samuel and Harriet Newell, and two young men friends who were spending the night on board, talked exultingly together of their high hopes for a great work to be achieved in Christ's name in the needy countries of the ancient East. They sang hymns from an old singing-book long since forgotten, and they prayed in the "quietness and confidence" that was their daily strength. Ann Judson, shiny eyed and triumphant, sang and talked with almost her usual animation.

Somewhat quieter than the others was the youngest of their number, Harriet Newell. Her thoughts clung wistfully to the mother away over the snowy fields in Haverhill town.

Late in the evening she wrote her a letter to be sent back by the pilot-boat on the morrow:

Here am I, my dear mother, on board the brig *Caravan* in a neat little cabin. . . . I have at length taken leave of the land of my forefathers and entered the vessel which will be my place of residence till I reach the desired haven. Think not, my dear mother, that we are now sitting in silent sorrow, strangers to peace. O, no; though the idea that I have left you, to see you no more, is painful indeed, yet I think I can say that I have found the grace of my Redeemer sufficient for me — his strength has been made perfect in my weakness. We have been engaged in singing this evening, and can you believe me when I tell you that I never engaged in this delightful part of worship with greater pleasure? . . . I never shall repay you, my dear mother, for all the kindness and love you have shown me thus far in life. Accept my sincere thanks for every favor, and O, forgive me for so often causing you pain and anxiety. May the Almighty reward you a hundred-fold for your kindness to me. And now, my dear mother, what more shall I say but ask you to pray for me and engage other Christians to do the same. . . . It is late — I must retire — dear mother, adieu.

The following morning, the nineteenth of February, a little after sunrise, the *Caravan* spread her sails to the wind and steered her course straight out to sea. The tall chimney at the entrance of the harbor was a landmark long to be distinguished as it traced a black perpendicular against the snowy New England hills. But by and by it vanished into dim space and the great, gray ocean was all around.

Chapter 5

PERPLEXITIES ON
EVERY SIDE

INSIDE a musty old tavern made of mud and straw, on the banks of the Hoogly River in India, a young woman waited in lonely suspense. The desolateness of her attitude might have revealed her as a stranger in a strange land, even had her brown hair and fair skin not marked her instantly as different from the richly brunette women of India. In beauty, however, she belonged among the loveliest in that land of lovely women, and the sad anxiety in her eyes added a softened appeal to her charm.

For the first time since she had landed in India five months before, Ann Judson found herself alone and unprotected among the strange, dark people of the country, with their stranger tones and gestures. Where her husband was and when he would come, she did not know. They had been separated sixteen miles up the river when they received the government order to leave the ship in which they had taken flight from Calcutta two days previously. Here she was, without escort, with only a few rupees in her purse, only a few words of the language at her command, the old thatched tavern her only place of refuge, and even its hospitality uncertain. Her father's house in Bradford seemed millions of miles away, as if it were upon another planet, and her girlhood life in the New England village almost like another existence.

This was the solid reality of missionary experience of which she had vaguely dreamed in the early days of her engagement to Adoniram Judson. "These are the trials which attend a missionary's life and which I anticipated," she said to herself, "and which, with God's help, I am ready to meet."

It was a series of disappointing adventures that had led up to Ann's desolate situation in the river tavern. When the American missionaries landed in Calcutta in June, 1812, the East India Company had promptly turned its hostile eye upon them and determined to force them out of the country. This company was a trading corporation that at that time controlled Great Britain's policy in India. Its officials had no welcome for missionaries, because it was feared that any attempt to interfere with the idolatrous religion of the native peoples would breed rebellion to British rule. Moreover, a large revenue poured into the treasury of the company from protection given to idol worship, so that the heathen religion was financially profitable. A year later, by the efforts of some Christian men in England, the charter of the East India Company was amended in its passage through Parliament to insure toleration to missionaries in India.

In 1812, however, the little groups of American pioneers arriving by the *Caravan*, and six weeks later by the *Harmony*, felt the full brunt of government opposition, aggravated by the hostile relations then existing between England and America because of the second war between the two countries.

Upon landing in India the Judsons and Newells had been invited to Serampore to visit the English Baptist missionaries until their companions should arrive by the *Harmony* and locations for the new missions be determined. William Carey, the first English foreign missionary, with his colleagues, Marshman and Ward, had, by persistent struggle, built up a wonderful missionary enterprise in the town of Serampore on the Ganges, fifteen miles from Calcutta. Here the newcomers spent ten happy, absorbing days observing the customs of the country and trying to decide, with the help of the older missionaries, where they would settle.

Burma had been the land of desire for Adoniram Judson since his student days at Andover, when he had read Colonel Symes's *Embassy to Ava* and his imagination had responded to its glowing pictures of Oriental life. But Burma was a forbidden territory to missionaries, said Dr. Carey, because of the cruel despotism of its government and the brutal savagery of its inhabitants. Two Englishmen had attempted a mission there, but had abandoned it as hope-

· 37 ·

less. Dr. Carey's son, the only missionary then in Burma, had been obliged to take refuge for fifty days on an English frigate, and his return to the country had been on precarious terms. Burma presented a dismal prospect, but where should they go to escape the hostility of the East India Company and find a people who would listen to their message?

One July afternoon their deliberations met with a vigorous interruption. An official messenger arrived at Serampore bearing a summons for Mr. Judson and Mr. Newell to present themselves immediately at the police office in Calcutta. There, an order from the Governor-general was read to them, commanding them to *return to America* upon the very ship on which they had come, the *Caravan*, then making ready for her westward voyage. Captain Heard had been refused a clearance from port unless he gave security that his missionary passengers would be taken on board.

What should they do? It was insufferable to think of going home before their work was even begun. The disappointment and humiliation were overwhelming, but the belief that God had sent them and meant them to remain was unshaken.

There seemed to be but one way of escape — to seek some other heathen country, outside the jurisdiction of the East India Company. So, with sudden, desperate purpose they asked permission to embark for the Isle of France. The Isle of France, now Mauritius, was five thousand miles southwest, near Madagascar. Their request was granted, and on the fourth day of August Samuel Newell and his frail wife sailed away from all their friends in a small ship bound for Port Louis, in the Isle of France. The vessel could accommodate but two passengers, and the Newells were chosen to go because Harriet's frail health made a home an urgent necessity.

Four months longer Adoniram and Ann Judson lingered in Calcutta, living in daily dread of summary dismissal from the country. Mr. Rolt, an Englishman, somewhat relieved their embarrassing predicament by offering the hospitality of his home. There, in his spacious English house, while waiting for a way out of their dilemma, the greatest of their many perplexities assailed them.

They were confronted by a troublesome problem that could not be evaded, and that pressed daily upon their minds for solution. On shipboard, while making the long voyage of four months from America to India, they had first grappled with the question of the Baptist belief as distinguished from that of the Congregationalists, and Mr. Judson's old convictions had become strangely disturbed. At first Mrs. Judson took the opposite side in argument and declared with her old independence, "If you become a Baptist, I will not."

During the first weeks on shore the question was silenced by the more urgent demand for home and shelter. But in the long summer days in Calcutta, in the seclusion of Mr. Rolt's library, the subject recurred with painful insistence, and they resolved to deal conscientiously and thoroughly with its claims. The result was that they felt themselves compelled by conviction to withdraw from the Congrega-

tionalists, with whom their lot had been cast since childhood, and to join the Baptists.

In those days communions were more sharply divided
than today, and to change from one to another usually
meant a heroic act of conscience. Especially for the pioneer
missionaries was it a difficult and brave decision. They could
hardly expect the continued support of the Congregationalists, nor could they confidently look to the Baptists for
financial aid, since that denomination was not organized for
missionary activity.

Where should they turn? Supporters and friends would
be likely to misinterpret their action. Even their own families, when removed by so great a distance, might find their
decision hard to understand and accept. Hardest of all,
they would probably have to be separated in future work
from their companions, those old schoolmates and friends
who had come to India with them. "A renunciation of our
former sentiments has caused us more pain than anything
which has ever happened to us through our lives," wrote
Mrs. Judson in a home letter.

One happy surprise came to relieve their downcast condition. To the amazement of all his associates, Luther Rice
quietly announced his intention to join the Baptists. In the
secrecy of his own thoughts he had been dealing with the
question, and his conclusion was thus reached inde-
pendently of outside influence. It was a great solace to
the Judsons in their lonely outlook to have the assurance of
his companionship in their new mission, wherever their
work might take them.

Another strong encouragement came from the splendid generosity of the missionaries at Serampore. They held a consultation and agreed to supply funds for the American missionaries out of their own treasury in case money did not arrive from America when needed. They would advance the sums required, and if the American societies could reimburse them, well and good; if not, they would count it a gift to the cause of Christ.

Mr. Rolt was unfailing in his interest and sympathy with the young people who had come so many thousands of miles from home on a mission of good will, and had met such a frosty reception at the hands of government authorities. They continued to be his guests until late in November, when one day, about Thanksgiving time at home in New England, a startling order was brought to the house in Calcutta. Mr. and Mrs. Judson and Mr. Rice were commanded by the government to embark at once for England upon a vessel of the East India Company. Their names were published in the newspaper lists of passengers on the England-bound ship. All hope of escape seemed to be cut off this time, but the two young men and one young woman were not ready to acknowledge themselves beaten by the whole East India Company, so again they tried to circumvent its order.

By some means Mr. Judson and Mr. Rolt discovered that a ship named the *Creole* would sail in two days for the Isle of France. They applied to the chief magistrate for a passport, but he refused them. They then asked the captain if he would take them on board without a pass. He replied:

"There is my ship; do as you please." With Mr. Rolt's assistance they secured coolies to carry their baggage, and at midnight stole like criminals through the deserted streets of Calcutta, through the gates of the dockyards, which, contrary to night rules, opened to admit them, and on board the forbidden vessel. The next morning the *Creole* sailed out of Calcutta harbor, down the Hoogly River toward the Bay of Bengal and the open sea.

For two days all was well on shipboard, but toward evening of the second day, a government dispatch overtook them, forbidding the pilot to proceed since there were passengers on the ship who had been ordered to England. The pursued passengers must needs leave the vessel at once, even in the darkness of evening, so the two young men entered a small boat to go on shore to a tavern about a mile away.

The captain, with the gallantry born of the sight of a lovely woman in distress, bade Mrs. Judson spend the night on the ship, where their baggage also would be allowed to remain. It would be quite safe for her, he assured her, even though an officer should come to search the boat.

Through the night and the next day the *Creole* lay at anchor waiting for orders. When evening came, Mrs. Judson also was forced to depart hurriedly for land. The owner of the ship heard of its detention and went to police headquarters to inquire the reason. There he was informed that "it was suspected there were persons on board whom the captain had been forbidden to receive." The ship could not proceed until it was proved that no such parties were among the passengers. Mrs. Judson hastened on shore in a small boat while the pilot wrote a certificate that the suspected persons were not on the ship.

At the tavern Mrs. Judson found her husband and Mr. Rice, and in tense anxiety they consulted as to their next move. What *should* they do? Escape on the *Creole* was now hopelessly blocked without a passport. Return to Calcutta would be but a confession of defeat. Where was the way out of this labyrinth of perplexities?

Mr. Rice decided to start for Calcutta at once, to make one more effort to secure a pass. Mr. and Mrs. Judson spent the night and the next day at the tavern, watching in vain for a message from the ship where their baggage still remained, and dreading lest every European in sight was spying upon their movements.

Mr. Rice came back from Calcutta to report another refusal. The owner of the ship was in high dudgeon because his vessel was delayed so long on their account. "Perplexed on every side, yet not unto despair," because, as Harriet Newell once said: "He who takes care of the ravens will not forsake his own children in the hour of their affliction."

Another uneasy night at the tavern and in the morning a disquieting message from the captain of the *Creole! He* was permitted to sail, but *they* must remove their baggage from the ship at once. It seemed unwise to linger longer at the tavern, so they decided to journey on to another little Indian inn sixteen miles down the river.

It would be hazardous for the two men to show themselves on the prohibited vessel, so Mrs. Judson went alone on board the *Creole* and made arrangements for the transfer of their baggage. As she could find no small boat, she asked the captain if the baggage might be left where it was until the next tavern was reached. Not only did he readily consent, but invited Mrs. Judson to make the journey herself on his vessel, saying that the river trip in a small craft would be exceedingly unpleasant.

Again she hurried on shore to notify her companions of this change of plan. For the second time Mr. Rice set out for Calcutta to secure passage, if possible, for Ceylon. Mr. Judson hired a boat for his own transportation down the river to the tavern appointed.

Meanwhile, Mrs. Judson returned to the *Creole* in the pilot's boat that he had courteously sent on shore for her use. It was an exciting and dangerous chase after the ship, which had slipped rapidly down stream with the tide. The river was rough because of the high wind, and the tropical sun blistering in its rays of heat. The native rowers hoisted a sail so large that repeatedly it tilted the boat on one side. To allay the fears of their fair lady passenger they kept repeating, *"Cutcha pho annah, sahib, cutcha pho annah."* ("Never fear, Madam, never fear.")

At last they came safely alongside the large vessel, hastened on board, and soon stopped opposite the uninviting old tavern to which Mrs. Judson must go alone. Again the pilot offered his boat to convey her to shore. There, with all speed, she arranged for another boat to go out to the *Creole* to remove their baggage. Finally, the necessary business done, she turned hesitatingly toward the thatched

tavern that must harbor her, welcome or not, until her husband should arrive.

Longer than it has taken us to recount these adventures, Ann Judson had to watch and wait for the coming of her husband. Several hours dragged by before he appeared at the entrance of the tavern and eagerly sought his wife. Thankfully the two greeted each other, their relief at their mutual safety overcoming for a time anxiety for the future.

Quickly, however, they began to strain every nerve of thought to find a way out of their present dilemma. Should they, after all, return to Calcutta and face the worst, or should they confide in the tavernkeeper and seek his assistance?

Anything seemed preferable to a retreat to the city that had exiled them, so they asked the innkeeper if he could help them secure a passage to Ceylon. He replied that a captain who was a friend of his was due on the morrow, and that very likely he might take them on his ship bound for Madras. Encouraged by this possibility and by the safe arrival of their baggage, they waited two days at the tavern, during which time Mr. Rice rejoined his companions.

On the third day the looked-for vessel anchored directly opposite the tavern. The innkeeper went on board to intercede on behalf of his fugitive guests, but returned with the refusal of the captain to receive them as passengers. Thereupon they resolved to interview the stubborn captain themselves and beg for leniency. With this slender hope in mind, they sat down to supper, when a letter was handed to them!

They felt as if an actual miracle had been wrought when they found that the letter contained a pass from the chief magistrate for embarkation on the *Creole* for the Isle of France. "Who procured this pass for us, or in what way, we are still ignorant: we could only view the hand of God and wonder." Thus wrote Mrs. Judson in a long home letter detailing her many adventures.

Then followed a frantic pursuit of the *Creole*, which they feared might be already out at sea, since she had three days' start. It was just possible that she might be anchored at Saugur, seventy miles down stream, at the entrance of the Hoogly River. At any rate, they must make the venture and hasten the pursuit.

As soon as darkness fell the three fugitives hurried into a small boat and pushed out against the tide for their race to safety. All that night Mrs. Judson watched with wide-open eyes by the side of her husband, who slept peacefully until morning.

The next day wind and tide sped them on their way, and by nightfall Saugur was in sight, with the masts of many ships at anchor. Was the *Creole* among them, or had she already crossed the invisible boundary between river and bay and sailed beyond recall? With eager eyes they scanned the boats and — joy to behold — there was the *Creole* in their midst! For two days she had been anchored at Saugur waiting for members of her crew. "I never enjoyed a sweeter moment in my life than that when I was sure we were in sight of the *Creole*," wrote Ann Judson to the Hasseltine house in Bradford.

Chapter 6

THE ISLE OF FRANCE

SOMETIMES it happens that the loveliest scene in nature becomes the background of the most woeful tragedy. The Isle of France, for natural beauty, was among the most charming of the islands of the Indian Ocean. Blue, blue sky was reflected in the waters of the reef-bound harbor, and filmy clouds brooded upon the summits of the mountains. Gleaming springs flashed like quicksilver down the shadowy mountainsides, and the scarlet and blue blossoms of the climbing plant hung from the dark cliffs. In the woods and valleys grew lemon and orange trees, date and coco palms, and a tangle of brightly-colored, fragrant flowers.

It was this setting of tropical verdure that Saint Pierre chose for his tragic and true tale, *Paul and Virginia*. It was in the city of Port Louis, at the foot of the mountain that sheltered in a rock-bound vale the cabin of Paul and Virginia, that, one hundred years later, Samuel and Harriet

Newell met the tragedy of their young lives. Here, also, Ann and Adoniram Judson came too late to succor their friends in their hour of need.

In January, 1813, after nearly two months of contrary winds and rough seas, the *Creole* sailed into the harbor of Port Louis and dropped anchor. On deck Mrs. Judson stood with her husband and Mr. Rice, gazing at the fairyland scene before them, wondering if there at last they would find the home they had sought so many months in vain, wondering, too, how soon they would greet Samuel and Harriet Newell and with them compare adventures of the past and prospects for the future.

As they lingered on the ship waiting for some means of transportation to shore, a young man came on board to welcome them, but so slow and reluctant was his step, so changed and haggard his face, they scarcely recognized their old friend Samuel Newell. Before he could speak Ann Judson read the tale that his sorrowful, beseeching eyes revealed. Harriet, his own beloved Harriet, had left him alone in the world. In broken snatches, then and later, he told his friends of his bitter loss.

The ship on which the Newells had taken passage from Calcutta the August before had been battered unmercifully by winds and waves, so that the voyage lengthened into three anxious months. Far out on the Indian Ocean a baby girl was born in the little cabin on the ship's deck and given her mother's name, Harriet Atwood. For a few days joy and hope abounded in the hearts of the parents, but speedily cold and rain fell upon the ill-fated ship, and the baby, unable to endure the exposure, died in her mother's arms. After the child's death Harriet showed the first signs of the fatal disease that rapidly consumed her life.

When at length the dreadful voyage was over and the belated ship came to port, a British surgeon and a Danish physician ministered to the sick wife, but to no avail. Gradually her strength waned until the last flicker of hope for her recovery vanished.

Night and day Samuel Newell sat by the bedside of his dear one trying to catch every precious word she spoke. Her thoughts seemed to dwell with perfect restfulness upon Christ and heaven, recurring sometimes to her mother across the seas in the Atwood homestead in Haverhill.

"Tell my dear mother," she said, "how much Harriet loved her. Tell her to look to God and keep near to him and he will support and comfort her in all her trials. Tell my brothers and sisters, from the lips of their dying sister, that there is nothing but religion worth living for. Tell them, and also my dear mother, that I have never regretted leaving my native land for the cause of Christ."

One afternoon in November, the blindness of death sealed Harriet's brown eyes, and there, in the little mud-walled cottage, she quietly breathed her last. Throughout that awful night Samuel Newell watched beside his dead, a Negro servant his only companion in the silent house.

In a land of strangers, without one friend to weep with him, he followed the body of his wife to the graveyard of Port Louis. There, in the heathy ground, under an evergreen tree that suggested her New England home, was buried the young woman who was the first American to give her life for the cause of Christ in the non-Christian world.

Ann Judson's thoughts turned mournfully toward that burial spot that was the symbol of her welcome in the Isle of France. Who could have thought that death would so speedily claim one of their little band, whose lives were all the more precious to one another because they were so few in number and so immeasurably far from home? With but small assurance that this far-away island was to be their permanent home, the Judsons settled themselves in Port Louis and waited for some unmistakable signs of God's guidance.

As they waited, they watched for opportunities to serve the need of the people about them. On Sunday Mr. Judson or Mr. Rice preached to the British soldiers stationed on the island. The governor was friendly and would permit a Christian mission to be established, even though he had received warning from the British government at Bengal to "keep an eye upon those American missionaries." Moreover, there was convincing evidence of the ignorance and degradation of the inhabitants of the island.

One evening there was a hideous commotion in the courtyard that adjoined the Judsons' house in Port Louis. A Negro slave stood with her hands tied behind her back while her mistress beat her unmercifully with a club.

Promptly Mrs. Judson opened her door and ventured upon the scene. In broken French she begged the cruel mistress to stop beating her slave. Surprised by the interruption and by the gentle beauty of the strange lady, the

woman ceased her blows but angrily insisted that the servant was very bad and had recently run away. Mrs. Judson
talked quietly with the enraged mistress until her anger
seemed to be appeased, although, as a parting taunt, she
hurled her club at the slave's head with such force that
blood ran down upon the girl's clothes. All night the poor
creature was left with her hands tied behind her back, and
in the morning she was released and set to work.

The second night the clank of an iron chain was heard as
it was dragged across the courtyard. From her quarters in
the neighboring house Mrs. Judson saw, to her horror, that
the heavy chain was intended for the unfortunate slave.
To one end of the long chain was fastened a ring large
enough to be locked around her neck, and to the ring were
attached two pieces of iron which would press against her
face on either side and prevent her eating. The slave girl
stood trembling as they prepared to put the chain upon her.

At mere sight of her servant the mistress fell into a furious temper and began beating her as she had done the night
before. Again she was intercepted by Mrs. Judson.

"Your servant is very bad, no doubt," she said in her
pretty foreign accent, "but you will be very good to forgive
her."

Again the mistress drew back her club and finally, yield-
ing to entreaty, consented to forgive her slave and release
her from the punishment decreed. Emphatically she declared that pardon was granted, not out of any consideration for the slave, but simply because the American lady
requested it.

The terrified Negress was made to understand the terms of her release. Whereupon she knelt and kissed the feet of the fair white lady who had saved her, crying, "*Merci, madame, merci, madame.*"

Mrs. Judson could scarcely keep back her tears as she received the gratitude of the slave girl. She returned to the house happy-hearted because she had delivered one poor slave from a night of physical misery, but at the same time brooding sadly upon the spiritual misery that she saw daily in the faces of the people about her.

In March Mr. and Mrs. Judson were left alone in the Isle of France. Mr. Newell departed for Ceylon, away from the scene of his desolated life, and Mr. Rice actually sailed for America, the dear homeland that grew dearer every day. He was going back to tell the Baptist churches what letters could never adequately tell, that the heathen peoples he had seen were in desperate need of the knowledge of Christ, and that over there in distant Asia a young man and his wife were eagerly waiting to be adopted as the first missionaries of the Baptist denomination in America.

Meanwhile, those two young people lingered in Port Louis watching daily for some indication to tell them the place in which God had appointed them to live and labor. There was some promise of usefulness in the Isle of France, yet when they compared its population with that of other regions of the Orient they could not feel warranted in remaining.

The ancient East contained hundreds of millions of people, but Christian missionaries were not many more in number than the original group of twelve whom Christ commissioned to "go and make disciples of all the nations." Among "all the nations" of Asia where should they find a strategic place to establish a Christian mission? This was the anxious query that pervaded the spring days in the tropic island, and to which the summer gave an answer unexpected and unwelcome.

Chapter 7

A HOME AT LAST

WHEN Nancy Hasseltine was a gay, restless schoolgirl her mother once reproved her by saying, "I hope, my daughter, you will one day be satisfied with rambling." Little did the girl or mother dream how literally those words would be fulfilled. For a whole long year following the day in June when Ann Judson and her husband went on shore from the *Caravan* in Calcutta harbor, they knew little else but rambling — incessant traveling from place to place in weary, anxious search for some spot they would be allowed to call home.

They had now embarked from the Isle of France, intending to settle in Pulo Penang, or Prince of Wales' Island, in the Malacca Strait, which, since its purchase by the British, was receiving a large population of Hindus, Chinese, Burmans, and Siamese. No ship sailed directly from the Isle of France to Penang, so it was necessary that they take passage to Madras, expecting to proceed from that port to the Malacca Strait.

Early in June the travelers found themselves again in the domains of the East India Company, which twice before had decreed their exile. Their arrival in Madras was promptly reported to the police and the report forwarded to the supreme government in Bengal.

It was plainly to be seen that as soon as a return message could reach Madras they would be arrested and ordered to England. Escape must be immediate and final. Several vessels lay at anchor in the Madras roads and Mr. Judson anxiously inquired their destination, knowing that the direction of those ships soon to sail must determine the fate of himself and his wife and the new mission.

Alas, only one would sail in time and that one was destined for the port most dreaded, most formidable in all the Eastern world, Rangoon, Burma! The question was now brought to an issue decisive and unescapable. Burma it must be or Europe and home! Which? Yes, which? Should they venture into that wild, barbaric country, outside a civilized government, inside a despotic monarchy of the most merciless variety? All their new-found friends in Madras protested against it. The test was stupendous for two young people not yet twenty-five years of age, and it threw them upon God as their only dependence.

About this time the diary of Ann Judson bore a troubled entry:

June 20th. We have at last concluded, in our distress, to go to Rangoon, as there is no vessel about to sail for any other place ere it will be too late to escape a second arrest. O, our heavenly Father, direct us aright! Where wilt thou have us go? What wilt thou have us do? Our only hope is in thee, and to thee alone we look for protection. . . . I have been accustomed to view this field of labor with dread and terror, but I now feel perfectly willing to make it my home the rest of my life. . . . To-morrow we expect to leave this place and the few friends we have found here. Adieu to polished, refined, Christian society. Our lot is not cast among you, but among pagans, among barbarians, whose tender mercies are cruel. Indeed, we voluntarily forsake you and for Jesus' sake choose the latter for our associates.

The voyage to Burma proved to be every whit as disagreeable as anticipations of the country had been. It was the most distressing and dangerous journey they had ever experienced, not excepting Mr. Judson's trip to England when he was captured by pirates.

First of all, a disastrous catastrophe took place at the outset of the voyage. Because of Mrs. Judson's frail health her friends in Madras had procured a European woman servant to accompany her to Burma. This woman appeared to be in normal condition when she went on board the ship, but within a few hours after sailing she fell upon the floor writhing in convulsions. Mrs. Judson labored over her, trying by every means in her power to restore her, but all her efforts failed and after a few gasps the serving woman died.

The shock of the sudden death, together with the violent exertion to save the woman's life, threw Mrs. Judson into such an excruciating sickness that she was brought very close to death herself. In their uncomfortable quarters on shipboard the experience was the heaviest hardship they had yet borne.

The ship *Georgianna* was a "crazy" old craft, dirty, miserable, and unseaworthy. There was no stateroom for the two passengers except such as was made by canvas protection on deck. The wind was blustering and the waves choppy. The boat tossed incessantly, its motion bringing agonizing pain to the sufferer on deck.

No physician and no medicines were at hand to relieve her distress. The captain was the only other person on board who could speak English, as the *Georgianna* was a Portuguese ship. Mr. Judson was doctor, nurse, and companion. As he sat by the prostrate form of his wife, helpless to mitigate her pain, he realized something of the agony of spirit that Samuel Newell had endured as he watched, unfriended and alone, by the deathbed of Harriet in the Isle of France.

Apparently, there was but one way to save the life of Ann Judson, and that way seemed to be the last and greatest of impossibilities. If the tossing boat could be quiet for one hour relief might come that would lead to recovery. Then it was that God's watchful care over his own was beautifully manifested, just as Harriet Newell trustfully said: "He who takes care of the ravens will not forsake his own children in the hour of their affliction."

The captain came on deck to inform his passengers that they had failed to make the Nicobar Island, where it was intended to take on a cargo of coconuts, and that they were in imminent danger of being driven upon the Andaman

Islands. To escape this fate he would have to steer his vessel through a narrow strait between two of the islands, where he had never been before and that was reputed to be a region of great terror for men and ships. The coasts were said to be inhabited by cannibals who would promptly kill and eat everyone on board if they got a chance. Moreover, the channel was beset with perilous black rocks as deadly to passing ships as great icebergs should they happen to collide.

With these gruesome possibilities ahead, the ship entered the channel, when suddenly the wind ceased and the water became perfectly calm! The islands cut off the wind so completely that the narrow passage was like a sheltered haven, and the moving vessel almost as quiet as a house on land. The stillness brought immediate relief to Mrs. Judson and to her husband the first shining hope of her recovery. The dreaded rocks and cannibals were soon left behind and the ship, under more favorable winds, sailed steadily on toward port.

But what a port! It was the thirteenth day of July when the *Georgianna* entered the harbor of Rangoon, Burma. Dismal, doleful, forbidding, funereal — all the unpleasant adjectives in the dictionary could hardly do justice to the city of Rangoon in 1813, especially as it was seen from approaching vessels.

Reaching away from the water's edge was a vast, flat swamp, "a sludgy, squdgy creek," with tumble-down bamboo huts raised on poles above the ground. Everything in sight was dilapidated, neglected, filthy. For the first time in their travels Mr. and Mrs. Judson saw before them a country in its primitive, barbaric condition, untouched by European civilization. The prospect sent a stab of terror into their souls.

Toward evening Mr. Judson went on shore to reconnoiter, but came back to the ship more cast down than his wife had ever seen him. The night of their arrival in Rangoon marked the bluest experience of all their lives, so they both agreed and recorded in their diaries and letters. Afterwards they thought that they ought to have rejoiced that first night to find themselves actually at the haven of their long desire, a thoroughly heathen country, and moreover, one which did not promptly dismiss them from its shores. But at the time, so heavy was the burden of loneliness and homesickness that their one wish was for speedy death to remove them from the hardships of earth.

Sharing each other's distress, the husband and wife prayed together and committed themselves wholly to the care of their watchful God, and by and by peace came to their troubled spirits. "Although I have cast them far off among the heathen, and although I have scattered them among the countries, yet will I be to them as a little sanctuary in the countries where they shall come."

The next morning preparations were made to go on shore to the city they must learn to call home. Mrs. Judson was not able to walk, as she had not yet left her bed for so long as half an hour. There was no means of conveyance except a horse, which of course she could not ride. Someone's ingenuity found a way at last and she was carried off the ship in an armchair borne by means of bamboo poles on the shoulders of four natives.

Into the miserable, dirty town, with its bamboo and teak houses and its muddy creeks, the coolies carried their precious burden, until, in a shady spot, they halted and set down the chair. Instantly, crowds of Burmans flocked around to gaze at the strange foreign *woman*. Englishmen were no novelty in the streets of this Burmese seaport, but Englishwomen were seldom seen and were objects of undisguised curiosity.

Involuntarily, Mrs. Judson's head drooped with sickness and weakness, and thus some native women ventured near enough to peer under her bonnet into the pale, lovely face. To their wide-eyed scrutiny she returned a friendly smile, to which they responded with a loud laugh.

As the coolies lifted the chair to proceed, the onlookers gave a lusty shout which seemed to amuse the foreigners. On they went to the Rangoon customhouse, which was a small, open shed, in which, upon mats on the ground, sat several Burmese custom officials. Mr. Judson was submitted to a thorough search, after which request was made that a Burmese woman be allowed to search Mrs. Judson, to which she obligingly agreed. This ordeal over, the little party moved on to the mission house outside the city gates, built by the English Baptists, which was to be home for the American missionaries.

Where now are the green hills and sunny, white homesteads of New England? Are they but phantoms of memory? And where, yes, where is that blithe, beautiful girl, with her rosy cheeks and brown curls, who went gaily forth to the new academy in Bradford, her thoughts filled with the good times in which she was always the merry leader? Is she, too, a phantom of the past? Or has Nancy Hasseltine found her real self in the heroic, sacrificial life of Ann Judson?

Chapter 8

"BY THE OLD
RANGOON PAGODA"

RANGOON was a city of importance in the Burmese Empire despite its dilapidated appearance. Besides a population of many thousand, it was the government city of an extensive province, ruled by a viceroy who was a high official in the kingdom. Two miles north of the city rose one of the landmarks of Burma, the great Rangoon Pagoda, or Golden Temple of Buddha, visible for twenty miles round about. It was a tall, glittering structure, grotesque in its golden ornamentations and colossal in its proportions.

At the season of the great feast of Gotama or Buddha, multitudes of people came in boats on the river from long distances to worship and present offerings at the famous pagoda that was supposed to contain a relic of Buddha. Thus Rangoon was honored, perhaps second to Ava, the royal city, for its government seat and its sacred shrine.

In years to come it was destined to rank among the first seaports of the Orient, because of its commanding location upon a branch of the great Irrawaddy River. Yet, in 1813, for all its governmental prestige, for all its pretentious pagoda, it was still a miserable, dirty, unsanitary town, with its glorious possibilities of navigation and vegetation unutilized and even unimagined.

One day Ann Judson climbed the flight of steps leading to the pagoda and was allowed to walk about the platform. The scene appeared to her like fairyland run wild. The enchanted castles and ruined abbeys that haunted the pages of storybooks she had read seemed to come to life before her eyes. Fantastic images of Buddha, of angels and demons, elephants and lions, added barbaric picturesqueness.

Sometimes, as Mrs. Judson looked up at the towering structure from the distance of her own home outside the city gates, the polished spire among the trees suggested the white steeples of New England. Then would come a swift realization of the awful distance, not only in miles, but much more in character, between the New England church and the Burmese pagoda. Just as the meetinghouse was the symbol of the simple, straightforward life of the early American settlers, this grotesque structure symbolized the falsehood and degradation of the inhabitants of the ancient East.

In the streets and outskirts of Rangoon the two American residents found sufficient evidence of the wretched condition of the Burmese people. Many sick and diseased folk begged daily their few grains of rice and crept back to their only habitation, a piece of cloth stretched on four bamboos un-

derneath a shade tree. Others bowed under a heavy yoke of toil, earning thereby but a meager pittance, the larger part of which was snatched away by a greedy government.

It was part of the government system to pay no fixed salaries to its officers but to expect them to extort by taxation from the people the means for a luxurious living. The viceroy, or governor of a province, was popularly known as an "eater," since his function seemed to be to devour the possessions of his subjects. Each petty officer divided his spoil with the viceroy, and he in turn with the king, whose revenues were unfailing.

The king's word was absolute law in Burma, so that even a high official might be beheaded at a moment's notice. At one time an officer of the highest rank was seized by the public executioner and laid on the ground by the side of the road with a heavy weight upon his chest and the meridian sun blazing relentlessly upon him. After the king's wrath was thus appeased the man was restored to his former high position. The only way to escape punishment, whether innocent or guilty, was to pay large bribes to the viceroy. Thus everybody was afraid of everybody else, and consequently nobody told the truth.

"We cannot live without telling lies," they said.

Robberies were outrageously daring and frequent, especially in times of famine, when almost every night houses were broken into and thefts or murders committed. The mission house, where the Judsons lived, was particularly exposed to attacks of robbers and wild beasts because of its location outside the city walls. Moreover, in the vicinity was the place of public execution and of deposit for the refuse of the city.

It was a gruesome locality, but the immediate surroundings of the house were unexpectedly pleasant. Belonging to the property was an enclosed garden abounding in delicious fruits, such as oranges, bananas, guavas, pineapples, and the jack fruit and breadfruit. The house itself was built of teakwood and, though left in an unfinished style inside, was large and fairly convenient.

It was a July morning in 1813 when the young American missionary walked beside the impromptu conveyance that carried his sick wife from the ship *Georgianna* to the mission house outside the gates of Rangoon. There was but one other missionary in Burma at the time, Felix Carey, son of the great William Carey of Serampore. He and his family occupied the Rangoon mission property, though during the summer when the Judsons arrived he was away in Ava on business for the king.

Mrs. Carey was a native of Rangoon and she, with her two children, received the new missionaries into her home. She could speak but little English, so friendly conversation did not brighten their first days in a strange land. Moreover, it was a difficult task for an Eastern woman to create the home comforts for a Western woman trained to such a different mode of life. To Mrs. Judson, accustomed to the savory cooking of New England, the Burmese food was a daily trial. Bread and butter and potatoes were constantly missed, and the rice and milk and curried fowl that formed the staple diet were always unsatisfying. Yet, "instead of mourning that we have no more of the comforts of life, we have great reason to be thankful that we have so many," wrote the undaunted Ann.

Considering the handicaps of food, climate, and discomforts, Mrs. Judson recovered her health with surprising rapidity, and never at any time did the man and woman become shaken in their firm intention to remain in heathen Burma. As Mr. Judson said, "We soon began to find that it was in our hearts to live and die with the Burmans." Through the many vicissitudes of the past year and a half they had learned the lesson that God is always on the side of those who do their duty, and that his help is mightier than any human aid or human need.

Immediately upon settling in their new home, Mr. and Mrs. Judson began to study the Burmese language, which, as a study, was worse than higher mathematics, Sanskrit, and Hebrew put together. To learn a dead language like Greek or Latin, or a living language like French or German, as it is taught in school or college today, is like kindergarten play compared with mastering a living, Oriental language, mastering it until it is as familiar as your native speech. Moreover, to attempt, as the Judsons did, to acquire a language without an adequate dictionary or grammar or even a teacher who understands a word of your own speech, and with dried palm leaves covered with obscure scratches your only textbook, such a task might well be reckoned among the twelve labors of Hercules. After studying Burmese for more than a year, Mr. Judson still insisted that if he had his choice of being examined in a Burmese book or in a book in the French language, which he had studied for about two months, he would without the least hesitation choose the French. So much for the intricacy of the Burmese language!

When the native teacher first came to the mission house he rebelled against accepting the missionary's wife as a pupil. In his country a teacher's skill was considered wasted if bestowed upon such an inferior being as a woman. But when he saw that the husband was as eager to have his wife taught as himself, the teacher changed his tactics. From seven in the morning until ten at night the two determined students applied themselves to their task, going to bed as tired as they had ever been in all their lives.

Every day and all day they studied and studied, their only recreation being a walk in the garden or adjoining village, their only society found in each other. No word from home had yet reached them and they had been absent a year and a half. They were as famished as the starving people they saw about them when at last, a whole year later — *two years and a half after leaving America — the first home letter was laid in their hands!*

Mrs. Judson was the only woman in the Burmese empire who could speak English, and of course there were no Christians outside the mission household in the entire country of perhaps eight million people. This was the situation in which the woman found herself who, only a few years before, had been the merrymaker of Bradford, the girl whose beauty and cleverness were bywords in the valley of the Merrimac.

"Exposed to robbers by night and invaders by day," wrote this same girl in her journal, dated Rangoon, August 8, 1813, "yet we both unite in saying we never were happier, never more contented in any situation, than the present. We feel that this is the post to which God hath appointed us; that we are in the path of duty; and in a situation, which, of all others, presents the most extensive field of usefulness."

On the nineteenth of September, 1813, the two young missionaries, man and wife, partook together of the sacrament of the Lord's Supper, just as Samuel and Harriet Newell had united in the sacred service on the Isle of France the Sabbath before Harriet's death. Thus, in the mission house of Rangoon, with two lonely foreigners as participants, was born the Baptist church of Burma that today, a hundred and thirty-six years later, numbers 177,704 people in its membership and almost two thousand church organizations.

Among her early experiences in Rangoon, one of the most entertaining befell Mrs. Judson on the day she made her first call upon the wife of the viceroy, introduced by a French lady who lived in the city and was a frequent visitor at the government house. When the two guests arrived her highness had not yet arisen and they must await her pleasure. Meantime, the secondary wives of the viceroy diverted and amused them. They gathered like so many children around the two foreigners, examining their clothes, trying on their gloves and bonnets, and manifesting the most absurd curiosity.

At last the vicereine appeared, clad in rich Burmese attire and smoking a long, silver pipe. As she entered the room the other wives retreated to a respectful distance and crouched on the floor, not daring to speak unless addressed.

The honored first wife went forward to greet her guests and looked interestedly into the face of the beautiful stranger, the wife of the American teacher. Graciously she took her by the hand and led her to a seat upon the mat where she sat herself. One of her women in waiting presented a bunch of flowers and the vicereine removed several blossoms and ornamented Mrs. Judson's bonnet. She then plied her with many questions, especially concerning herself and her husband. Was she the first wife — meaning, was she the highest among the many wives she supposed Mr. Judson possessed, as did her husband? Did they intend remaining long in the country?

As they talked, the viceroy himself made a pompous entry into the room. Mrs. Judson literally trembled as she saw the huge, savage-looking man, with his long, heavy robe and his spear large enough for Goliath of Gath. This ferocious being was not only the ruler of their city, but a man high in favor at the proud court of Ava, a man who had only to nod his head and his subjects were pardoned or beheaded. Yet he too greeted the American lady with surprising graciousness, and asked her if she would drink some rum or wine.

As the guests rose to depart, the vicereine again took Mrs. Judson's hand, assuring her that she was happy to see her and bidding her come every day. She then escorted her visitors to the door, where they made their salaams and went away, the ordeal of a state visit in Burma over for that time.

Mrs. Judson had decided to make this call hoping thereby to gain a friendly acquaintance with the vicereine, which, in case of trouble with the Burmans, would admit her to the wife when Mr. Judson might be refused access to so august a personage as the viceroy himself. It remains to be seen how the charm of personality that was Mrs. Judson's heritage from girlhood won for her and her husband marvelous favors from the haughty nobility of Burma.

As a further precaution against danger in those unsettled times, Mr. and Mrs. Judson concluded, after six months' residence in the outskirts, to move into a house within the city wall. By so doing they would not only escape the unnecessary peril of robbers, but would come in closer contact with the people.

Only seven days after they left the mission house a band of fifteen or twenty desperate men, armed with knives, spears, and guns, attacked a house in the neighborhood, stabbed the owner, and departed with everything upon which they could lay their hands. The viceroy was so enraged at this bold plunder that he dispatched a chief officer with three hundred men to run down the thieves, with the result that seven robbers were put to death in most brutal fashion at the place of public execution.

Two months after this consternation spread through the city, another alarming event made the missionaries realize the uncertainty of existence in a heathen city. On a Sunday morning in March they walked out to the mission house to spend the day in quiet worship, as was their weekly habit. As they reached the house, a servant met them with the news that a fire was raging near the town. They hurried to the spot and found several houses burning briskly and the flames traveling in straight course toward the city. No efforts whatsoever were made to extinguish the fire, so there was reason to suppose the whole town would be consumed.

They hastened to the gates in order to enter the city and return to their house in time to remove their belongings, but lo, the gates were tightly closed! The poor, terrified people had shut the gates imagining, like foolish children, that they could thus shut out the flames, even though gates and walls were made wholly of wood.

Mr. and Mrs. Judson waited persistently until at last the gates were opened, and they hurried home to gather up their possessions and transfer them swiftly to the mission house beyond the zone of danger. All day the fire burned and burned until walls, gates, and houses innumerable were destroyed, and thousands of families were shelterless.

Thus, fire and robbers and dangers undreamed surrounded the two missionaries. But they went about the day's work undismayed. The golden shrine of Buddha, the old Rangoon pagoda, looked indifferently down upon the confused, distressed life of the people in the city, a silent witness of the powerlessness of Buddhism to save its followers. In the hearts of the two strangers in their midst burned the message of a God of love who alone could redeem the people of Burma from bondage.

Chapter 9

CHILDREN'S VOICES

IT was a January day in 1815, and preparations for departure were being made in the Judson household in Rangoon. Who could be going away, and where? Was it possible that they were both leaving Burma, having given up the mission as a hopeless task? That did not seem likely, and moreover the house was in its usual condition, its furnishings undisturbed.

One small trunk stood ready for removal to the ship, and presently Mrs. Judson came in dressed for a journey. Evidently she was the traveler, and her husband was to be left behind. Never since their marriage had they been parted for any length of time, and the peculiar circumstances of their isolated life had made them unusually dependent upon each other. Now, however, they must face a separation of two or three months at least, and the prospect was doleful indeed.

Mrs. Judson was about to sail for Madras to consult a physician, as her health was breaking down under the climate and privations of Burma, and no medical help was available there. She had refused to permit her husband to accompany her, as the new mission would suffer too much from the absence of them both. They were just beginning to make themselves understood in the Burmese language, and a few people were turning a listening ear to the story of a God who cared, though they but dimly comprehended the meaning of the strangely beautiful message. These first signs of a harvest to come were too precious to neglect, and the language must be all the more arduously studied in order to make the story plain to the bewildered people.

When it was decided that Mrs. Judson must go to Madras, she and her husband ventured one day into the presence of the viceroy of Rangoon with an unusual petition. They offered a small present, as was customary in Burma when seeking a favor from those in authority. The viceroy looked at their gift and inquired their business, whereupon Mr. Judson made bold to ask if a Burmese woman might be allowed to travel with Mrs. Judson across the Bay of Bengal to Madras.

This was indeed an extraordinary request, for did not the Burmese law prohibit the departure of a native woman from the country? Yet, marvelous to relate, the viceroy turned instantly to his writer and bade him make out an official order, giving the desired permit and eliminating all expense. It may be that something of the indomitable courage shining in the eyes of the frail woman before him appealed to the heart of the arrogant Burmese ruler and moved him to show such amazing condescension. At any rate the husband and wife, as they went away from the government house, felt humbly grateful to God for this encouragement at the outset of the journey.

The second dread was the thought of repeating that voyage across the Bay of Bengal that in the summer of 1813 had brought such unforgettable distress. Here, again, difficulties vanished, thanks to the gallant thoughtfulness of the ship's captain. Not only did he provide every necessity for his invalid passenger, but at the end of the voyage refused to accept payment for her passage.

Kindnesses on every side smoothed the way for the traveler, and none the less in Madras, where Ann Judson was well remembered. It had been nearly two years since she first came to Madras, there to be confronted with the horrible possibility of a home in Burma, that country of which she said she had heard such "frightful accounts." Though the prospect sent a shiver to her soul she had raised no protest, because, as people said of her, her loyal resolve was to go anywhere for Christ.

Such steadfastness is not lightly forgotten. When she came again to Madras her old friends received her into their homes and many delighted to do her honor. After a stay of six weeks she prepared to return to Burma, her health having perceptibly improved. Before leaving she sent a fee of seventy rupees to the physician who had attended her, which amount he promptly returned with the message that he was happy if he had been serviceable to her.

To Rangoon again, and how eager is the anticipation compared with the dreary forebodings of the first voyage to Burma! But who is this new, small passenger who goes with Mrs. Judson on board the vessel in Madras roads? A little girl stands by her side on the ship's deck and waves good-by to the friends on shore. Is she really going home with Mrs. Judson, and who can she be?

The mystery is easily solved if you will go back and meet some of Mrs. Judson's friends in Madras. During her two visits to the city she had experienced the kindness lavished upon missionaries by a young man named Von Someren, son of a major in the Dutch army. Often he would go down to the ships lying in Madras roads and insist upon claiming the missionaries who arrived as his guests. He would entertain them in his spacious house, advise them in their business negotiations, and speed them on their way up country or across seas.

In his home lived three orphan children, small cousins who had been left to his guardianship after the death of their parents. The youngest, Emily Von Someren, became very dear to Mrs. Judson, and when she thought of returning to Burma she longed to take the little girl with her. One day she made known her desire to Mr. Von Someren, and willingly he entrusted his ward, then seven years old, to the care of the woman he admired so deeply. Thus it came about that a small companion sailed back to Burma with Mrs. Judson.

Meanwhile, over in Rangoon a young man was working unceasingly, that he might in some measure forget the loneliness of his deserted home. From early morning until late evening he gave himself to language-study, his only respite being a conversation with the natives, which was really study in another form. There was scarcely a single person in the Burmese empire with whom he could talk sympathetically as friend to friend, and with whom he could enter into the deeper fellowship of prayer. His loneliness was enormous, and accentuated by contrast the richness of his companionship with the wife who shared so completely his interests and his great absorbing purpose. When her ship should sail into the harbor, the joy of living would come again into his heart.

Thus, when the spring days returned, new signs of life and activity returned also to the mission house in Rangoon. A woman's step, buoyant with the rebound of health, was heard about the house and tones of a childish voice reached the open, veranda-like room where Mr. Judson and his teacher sat at study. The dry old Burmese language became newly vitalized by the accompaniment of these home-like sounds.

Mrs. Judson had long ago taken upon herself the entire management of the household, that her husband might be left free for uninterrupted study. Her own lessons thus became interspersed with frequent digressions into household affairs, but these very digressions proved in the end her quickest means of acquiring a vocabulary. Often in her contact with the servants she would be obliged to talk Burmese all day.

The small Emily picked up Burmese words and phrases

day by day, until she too could speak the language and sing the songs. Although she lived in the country but six years, to the end of her life she could speak and write Burmese. One hymn that she frequently sang in after life always brought the tears to her eyes, though she could never tell why.

So those busy days of spring and summer led on to an autumn of surpassing happiness. As a forerunner of the great joy before them, good news came traveling across the seas from America to bring thanksgiving into the little household in Rangoon. At last, after three years of waiting, came the assurance that the Baptist churches of America had accepted Mr. and Mrs. Judson as their first missionaries and assumed responsibility for their support. A burden also was lifted from the English missionaries at Serampore, who all this time had been supplying funds for the two Americans, according to their generous promise, but out of meager resources.

Not in vain had Luther Rice sailed back to his native land to tell the story of what his eyes had seen in the needy countries of the Orient. In May, 1814, a second history-making assembly had been held in the United States similar to the eventful gathering in Bradford in June, 1810. From Massachusetts to Georgia the Baptist ministers had rallied their forces in conference at Philadelphia and had there organized the second foreign missionary society of America, known originally as the Triennial Convention, later as the American Baptist Foreign Missionary Society.

The new mission board not only guaranteed support for

Mr. and Mrs. Judson, but held out the hope that some glad day other missionaries would be sent to labor beside them. Perhaps in some wonderful future the Baptist denomination of America might accept from the hands of its pioneer missionaries the whole country of Burma to develop for the great King, just as formerly the governments of Europe received from the claims of their pioneer discoverers whole territories in North America to develop for the sovereigns at whose will they had gone across the Atlantic.

There in the frontier home in Rangoon two lonely settlers were comforted by the knowledge that they were not forgotten by Christians in America. This glad sense of relief prepared the way for the blessing that came into their home on the eleventh day of September, when a little son was born, the only child of foreign parents in the city of Rangoon.

Although no doctor or nurse could be secured for the young mother, her husband ministering to all her needs, two weeks' time found her writing home, "Since the birth of our little son my health has been much better than for two years before. I feel now almost in a new state of existence. Our hands are full, and though our prospects in regard to the immediate conversion of the Burmans are dark, yet our trust in God is strong." In that same letter, after wishing that her mother might see her sprightly little boy, she went on to say, "We hope his life may be preserved and his heart sanctified, that he may become a missionary among the Burmans."

Even his name embodied his parents' hopes for his manhood, for he was named in memory of a dauntless pioneer missionary in the New England colonies, Roger Williams. Into every day of that autumn and winter the baby Roger, by his sunny presence, brought something of the spell and brightness of Christmas. He was the plaything, pet, and cherished companion of his busy parents, and, baby that he was, he seemed to feel in his little heart a return of the affection lavished upon him.

Often he would lie for hours on a mat by Mr. Judson's study table, content if only he could see his father's face. If his mother or father passed his cradle without taking him up, his blue eyes would follow them wistfully to the door and fill with tears, so that, constrained by the sadness of that little face, they would have to turn back to the cradle. When study hours were over they hastened to find Roger to take him into the garden for exercise and for their own joyous recreation. There was no such specter as loneliness existent when the baby was their companion.

Thus the winter days sped happily by, but when spring came again anxiety crept gradually into the mother's heart. Every night a touch of fever flushed the baby's small body, but since the daytime found him apparently healthy and active, they hoped the fever would disappear with that bugbear of babyhood, teething.

One morning, after his mother had taken him from his cradle, he coughed violently for half an hour. A high fever followed and continued through the day, though giving place on the morrow to refreshing sleep. The third day the cough and fever returned and a Portuguese priest, the only person of medical pretensions in the place, was summoned.

He prescribed some simple remedies, but they brought no relief to the strange distress in the baby's throat, which caused such hard breathing it could be heard some distance away.

During the fourth night the mother sat beside her sick child until two o'clock, when she was so fatigued that the father relieved her watch. He gave the little fellow a drink of milk, which he took with eagerness and then fell asleep in his cradle. For half an hour he slept quietly, when, without a struggle, his breathing ceased and the baby Roger was gone.

In the afternoon of that same day a procession of forty or fifty Burmese and Portuguese followed the heartbroken parents to a little grave in an enclosure of mango trees in the garden. All who knew the "little white child," as the vicereine called him, strove to express their sympathy.

A few days later her highness came with all the pomp of her high position to proffer condolences. If the degree of her sympathy was proportioned to the size of her retinue, it was large indeed, for two hundred officers and attendants followed in her train.

When the sad-faced mother came to greet her guest, the vicereine smote her breast, saying, "Why did you not send me word that I might have come to the funeral?" Mrs. Judson replied that she did not think of anything at the time, so great was her distress. Whereupon the Burmese noblewoman tried sincerely to comfort a sister woman in grief, bidding her not to weep, turning also to Mr. Judson and cautioning him lest the sorrow destroy his health, which all too evidently was on the decline.

Not forgetting her duties as hostess, Mrs. Judson served her guest with tea, sweetmeats, and cake, which seemed to give her pleasure. All the while she was longing for the chance to serve the deep life needs of the Burmese vicereine who, in all her visits to the government house, had manifested such a friendly spirit, such a cordial welcome toward the wife of the American teacher. If only she could return her kindness by leading her to accept the greatest of all gifts, even God's Christmas Gift to his human children!

One lovely spring day, a short time after the vicereine's call at the mission house, a gracious invitation proceeded from her highness to the American family in Rangoon. Would they become her guests on a trip into the country to benefit their health and to "cool their minds," as she expressed it? They readily consented and presently a tall elephant with a howdah upon his back appeared at the gate of the mission house for their conveyance.

A long, imposing procession formed and wended its way toward the woods. Thirty men, with spears and guns in their hands and red caps on their heads, led the march. Directly behind them walked a monstrous elephant caparisoned with a gilt howdah, in which sat the tall, graceful figure of the vicereine, clad in red and white silk. In the place of honor behind her ladyship rode the American guests, followed by three or four elephants carrying the vicereine's son and government officers. At the rear came a lordly retinue, two or three hundred strong, the men and women retainers of the government house.

Through the woods the elephants trudged with soft,

"squdgy" tread, breaking down, at the command of their drivers, the small trees that obstructed progress. In the midst of a beautiful garden, luxuriant with wild, tropical growth, the procession halted, and under a wide-reaching banyan tree mats were spread for hostess and guests.

Again the vicereine sought by every means to divert and entertain her guests. She gathered fruit and pared it, plucked flowers and knotted them together, and presented these friendly tokens with her own hands as a mark of extreme favor. At dinner her cloth was laid beside that of her guests while she freely dispensed the bounty prepared.

In the evening the procession returned to the city, and a tall elephant stopped before the mission house for its riders to dismount. Since the death of little Roger, homecoming had lost its keen zest, its poignant expectancy. Yet out in the fragrant garden was a sheltered spot that bound their hearts more strongly than ever to the land of their adoption. There, underneath the mango trees, the mother often sat and wept by the grave of her first-born child. But even as the tears fell she wrote to a friend at home: "God is the same when he afflicts as when he is merciful; just as worthy of our entire trust and confidence now as when he entrusted us with the precious little gift."

Meanwhile, the little Dutch girl, Emily, crept all the more closely into the hearts of her adopted parents in their lonely life in Rangoon.

Chapter 10

ANN'S DILEMMA

CHRISTMAS day in a country where there is no Christmas! What a mockery of the jovial old saint who drives his reindeers down the chimneys of children's fancies! Has he access only to the hearts and homes of children of the West? Oh, Christmas, Christmas, with your radiant spell cast upon the winter days, where is the sign of your presence in this Burmese city, where the "temple bells are callin'," calling to the worship of an "idol made of mud"? In the great, golden pagoda, is there no place for the worship of a little Child born in a manger in Bethlehem?

In the mission house in Rangoon, Christmas in the year 1817 was celebrated by the disturbing events of departure. Again the little family group was to be broken by the absence of one of its members on an uncertain, compulsory journey. Before sunset, Mr. Judson would have sailed away from Rangoon, down the Irrawaddy River toward the sea, and then north along the coast to Chittagong, a port of Arracan, belonging to the dominions of the East India Company. It must be a momentous errand that would draw Adoniram Judson away from Rangoon at this critical stage in the development of the mission.

No less a motive than the welfare of the mission itself had impelled this curious journey into an unknown region. After four years of preparatory work, the time had come at last for a public proclamation of the gospel that hitherto the missionaries had expressed only by their daily lives, by private conversation, and recently by the circulation of two tracts and the book of *Matthew* printed in Burmese.

The knotty language had become so familiar to Mr. Judson that he was now ready to venture before a critical native audience. If, however, one Burmese Christian could stand by his side and declare in his native tongue to his own countrymen the beauty of the Christian religion, the appeal would be a hundred times more powerful. As yet there was no avowed disciple of Christ among the natives in Rangoon, although a number had shown an awakening interest.

In the port of Chittagong were said to be several converts, the remnant of an abandoned English mission in that region. It was likely that Mr. Judson could persuade one of these native Christians, who spoke Burmese, to return with him to Rangoon and assist him in his task of public preaching. Thus, when it was announced that a ship would sail on December 25 from Rangoon to Chittagong, to return in a few weeks, a unique opportunity presented itself.

Furthermore, a second purpose would be accomplished

by this sea voyage of about ten days in each direction. Renewed vigor would be imparted to Mr. Judson's worn-out body and mind. For nearly two years he had suffered acute pain in his eyes and head, caused by close study of the puzzling Burmese characters. For a period of four months he had not been able to read a page in a Burmese book, yet, during those very months, out of the knowledge already stored in his brain, he had compiled a grammar of the Burmese language! Twenty years later this grammar was published and pronounced by linguists to be a masterpiece in its brevity and completeness.

Once before during his sickness a sea voyage had been planned, but sudden, surprising news from Calcutta prevented departure. A new missionary and his wife had just arrived from America and would proceed to Rangoon by the next boat. Mrs. Judson would of course remain at home to welcome the newcomers, and an unexpected improvement in health detained Mr. Judson also.

In October, 1816, Mr. and Mrs. Judson had received into their home the first Americans who had ever crossed their threshold. Such eager inquiries about the homeland as filled those first wonderful days when isolation was exchanged for friendly companionship!

Mr. Hough, the new missionary, brought a timely present from the missionaries at Serampore — a printing press, the first to be seen in the Burmese Empire. So it came about, with Mr. Hough's knowledge of printing and Mr. Judson's knowledge of Burmese, that Christian publications were issued by the hundreds and thousands in the Burmese

language. Thus it also came about that Mrs. Judson and the small Emily were left in the midst of friends when Mr. Judson sailed away to Chittagong, expecting to return in the space of three months at the longest.

The New Year dawned, bringing with it tasks new and old. On every Sunday some twenty or thirty Burmese women gathered regularly at the mission house to listen to Mrs. Judson as she told them new, wonderful stories of a God who truly loved his human children. Sometimes their tongues found ready questions, or else expressed an intention to worship the true God and go no more to the idol temple. But their understanding and conviction were yet to be tested.

From the government house came unfailing signs of good will toward the American residents. Now and then an elephant appeared before the gate to convey them on excursions with the viceroy's family.

Her highness, the vicereine, showed unmistakable affection for Mrs. Judson, with whom she had several times permitted friendly conversation upon the subject of religion. From her hand also she had accepted the *Gospel of Matthew*, and the tract and catechism recently printed, even commanding that one of her daughters be taught to memorize the catechism that Mrs. Judson had written. But she gave no further indication of belief in the new religion, though Mrs. Judson watched eagerly for every token of deepening interest.

The last of January the coming of a visitor brought surprise and joy to the mission household. About a year before, when Mr. Judson was sitting with his teacher in his veranda-like room, a man of very respectable appearance, attended by a servant, had come up the steps and sat down before him. After a few preliminaries the stranger asked abruptly, "How long a time will it take me to learn the religion of Jesus?"

Mr. Judson had replied and then proceeded to ask him how he had heard about Jesus. The man answered that he had seen two little books. Mr. Judson then handed him the tract and catechism, both of which he recognized instantly and read sentences here and there, remarking to his servant, "This is the true God; this is the right way."

"More of this sort of writing," was his repeated request, to which Mr. Judson responded that he was even then translating a larger book that would be ready in two or three months.

"But," interposed the man, "have you not a little of that book done which you will graciously give me now?"

Mr. Judson folded a few pages of his unfinished manuscript and gave him the first five chapters of the book of *Matthew*. Immediately, his desire gratified, the man rose and went away.

For a year he had not returned, though Mr. Judson heard through a friend that he was reading his books "all the day" and showing them to every one who called upon him. He had been appointed governor of a group of villages in another region and came but seldom to Rangoon. Evidently upon his first opportunity he had resorted to the mission house.

In the course of their conversation Mrs. Judson asked him if he had become a disciple of Jesus Christ. "I have not yet," he replied, "but I am thinking and reading in order to become one. I cannot yet destroy my old mind. . . . Tell the great teacher when he returns that I wish to see him, though I am not a disciple of Christ." Having requested and obtained the remaining portion of the *Gospel of Matthew* and a supply of catechisms and tracts, he and his attendants went away.

Thus it was that encouraging signs gave zest to the activities of the mission, and Mrs. Judson's hope quickened in expectation of her husband's return. Any day now, his ship was due in port, for the time limit of three months had nearly expired. Mrs. Judson scanned the horizon for the first hazy lines of a ship's mast.

One day in March a vessel did indeed come creeping into the harbor, after twelve days' passage from Chittagong, but alas, it was not the boat in which Mr. Judson had sailed, and it brought most alarming news! Neither Mr. Judson nor the ship on which he had left Rangoon had been seen or heard of at Chittagong! This stray report brought by a native craft would not have been fully credited had it not been confirmed by messages that Mrs. Judson received at the same time from friends in Bengal.

Certain it was that her husband's ship had not reached its destination. Could it be that the course had been changed and the ship was yet safe in some unknown waters or port? This was a possibility, but on the other hand was the grim specter that frequently loomed larger than a possibility, that the ship on which Mr. Judson had sailed and all on board were lost. Oh, to know the truth, whatever the truth might be!

Into the midst of this agonizing suspense came annoyances from an unexpected quarter. An ugly-sounding order was received one afternoon bidding Mr. Hough appear at once at the courthouse to "give an account of himself."

This gruff message was so totally unlike any communication hitherto sent by the government that bewilderment and alarm spread quickly through the mission household. Mr. Hough hastened to obey the command, followed at a distance by a group of frightened teachers, servants, and other adherents of the mission.

As it was late when he reached the courthouse he was merely commanded to give security for his presence early the next morning, when, as they remarked with fiendish emphasis, "if he did not tell all the truth relative to his situation in the country, they would write with his heart's blood."

In such a predicament Mrs. Judson would ordinarily have appealed to the vicereine, but only a short time before, the friendly viceroy and his family had been recalled from Rangoon to Ava. His successor was but slightly acquainted with the Judsons, and moreover his family had been left behind in the royal city. It was contrary to Burmese etiquette for a woman to appear at court in the absence of the vicereine, consequently Mrs. Judson's tactful intervention was by custom prohibited. Mr. Hough could not speak Burmese with sufficient ease to permit him to appeal in person to the viceroy, so there was no recourse but for him to return on the morrow to the court session and to the uncertain fate there in store.

For two days he was held at the courthouse and forced to answer, through an interpreter, the most absurd questions, such as what were the names of his parents and how many suits of clothes did he possess, the answers to which were recorded with utmost formality. He was not even allowed recess long enough to procure food, but was incessantly subjected to examination.

On Sunday morning summons was again received to present himself at court that the inquiry might continue. Exasperated beyond endurance, Mrs. Judson determined to discover whether or not the viceroy was responsible for these maneuvers, or whether the subordinate officers were playing a shrewd game for bribes. Accordingly, her teacher wrote a petition addressed to the viceroy, stating their grievances, including the order to appear at court on their sacred day, and requesting that "it might be the pleasure of his highness that these molestations cease."

With fine disregard of Burmese custom Mrs. Judson prepared to go herself to the government house to intercede with the viceroy. Accompanied by Mr. Hough she entered the outer court and fortunately caught the eye of the viceroy as he sat in state surrounded by the officers of his court. He recognized her at once and with amazing condescension bade her come in and make known her request. Mrs. Judson handed the petition to one of the secretaries, who was promptly ordered to read it.

At its conclusion the viceroy inquired in a stern voice of the very officer who had been most aggressive in tormenting Mr. Hough, "Why has the examination of this foreign teacher been thus prolonged?" At the same time he gave a written order that Mr. Hough should not be disturbed upon his sacred day and that further annoyance should cease. Thus the petty officers were foiled of their purpose by an act that they did not dream a woman would dare even to attempt.

"Sweet are the uses of adversity" to a brave spirit like Mrs. Judson, but "ugly and venomous" was the form of its next approach. For the first time in the history of Rangoon a furious epidemic of cholera invaded the city, accelerated in its progress by the hottest and driest weather of the year. Only the coming of the rainy season would be likely to check the deadly march of disease.

From morning until night the death drum beat its gruesome lament, reminding Mrs. Judson and her companions of their imminent danger, but also of the unfailing watchfulness of their God. In very fact, throughout the long plague, not a person within the mission enclosure was touched by its ravages, though neighbors perished on every side.

Added to the wail for the dead was the mad din set up each night to expel the evil spirits who, the natives believed, stalked perpetually through the streets wantonly destroying life. A cannon fired at the government house gave the signal whereat every Burman began to beat upon his house with a club or anything that would make a noise. The uproar was hideous, and only a very deaf or stubborn spirit would have refused to depart, yet the disease remained as virulent as ever.

To one anxious woman the wail by day and by night was naught compared with the low, mournful cry of her heart for the return of her husband. Where in this whole Eastern world could he be, and when would he come home again?

When *could* he come? was the next question to torture Mrs. Judson's mind. Already rumors of war were adding to the confusion of disease. England was said to be at enmity with Burma and on the verge of bombarding the country. Was this the reason that no ships from English ports had entered the harbor in recent months? Did this account for the stealthy departure, one by one, of the boats anchored at Rangoon until but a single lonely craft was left? That too would be off to Bengal at the first opportunity, leaving the missionaries stranded in Rangoon with every kind of unnamed terror in prospect.

Mr. Hough believed it to be their duty to escape while there was yet opportunity. Mrs. Judson, on the other hand, was strongly averse to leaving the one spot in all the world where her husband knew she was to be found. To remain in Rangoon even in loneliness, war, and pestilence was her dominant desire and her felt duty. Yet how could Mr. Judson return to her in Burma if an embargo should be laid upon English ships? But where, oh, where could she find him in Bengal or the vast country of India? Should she go or should she stay? If she decided to go, she was in dread of missing her husband for months if not forever. If she decided to stay, he might be cut off from reaching her, and moreover her life would be seriously endangered. It was a dreadful dilemma, the biggest and most puzzling she had ever encountered in all her career.

At last, discouragement and perplexity battered down her first resolve, and with a heavy heart she made preparations to leave Rangoon. With the hope begotten of a great love she planned definitely upon meeting her husband in Bengal, and went so far as to engage his Burmese teacher to go with her that language study might be resumed. The teacher's courage failed, however, and he broke his engagement, fearing the embarrassment of his position should war be declared between Burma and Great Britain.

On the fifth of July, the mission house was left behind, while Mrs. Judson and Emily, with Mr. and Mrs. Hough, went on board the last remaining ship in the harbor. Even yet Mrs. Judson was not convinced of the wisdom of her decision. The old reluctance grew and grew even as the ship receded slowly and surely down the river toward the sea. Nothing could reconcile her to this enforced departure, but it was too late now to retrace her course. She seemed to be the victim of adverse circumstances, but usually her will was stronger than circumstances. Why not now? What was the meaning of this persistent set of her heart to return to Rangoon, just as in the journeyings of the Master his face was steadfastly set to go to Jerusalem?

The vessel was even now at the point where the river meets the sea, when the course was suddenly changed and directed toward the nearest harbor. Unseaworthy conditions had been discovered and the ship must be reloaded.

Here was Mrs. Judson's one and only chance for escape, and with determined voice she announced her intention to return to Rangoon. The captain agreed to send her back in a boat and to forward her baggage the next day.

It was evening when Mrs. Judson and her little companion, Emily, entered the city and sought out the house of the only Englishman left in Rangoon, where they spent the night. The next morning they went out to the mission house to the surprise and joy of all the Burmans left on the premises.

Alone with her little girl, among people of an alien race, in a disturbed, isolated city, Mrs. Judson wrote in her diary of July 14: "I know I am surrounded by dangers on every hand, and expect to feel much anxiety and distress, but at present I am tranquil, intend to make an effort to pursue my studies as formerly and leave the event with God."

Within two days of the return to Rangoon, a long lost vessel sailed into the harbor, even the very ship on which Mr. Judson had departed six months before! Mrs. Judson hastened to the captain to hear the news he brought of her husband.

It was only an unfinished tale he had to tell. The ship had not been able to make its intended port, Chittagong, and for three months had been tossed about in the Bay of Bengal without a haven. At last they had crept into Masulipatam, a port north of Madras on the coast of India, where Mr. Judson had left the ship to go to Madras, seeking speedy passage thence to Rangoon.

Beyond this point the captain could give no account of his

whereabouts, but to know that he had escaped shipwreck and was trying his best to return home brought a great lift of expectancy to Mrs. Judson's spirits and confirmed the wisdom of her decision to go back to Rangoon. This ship was the first to arrive from India in four months, but the fact of its coming indicated that war was not so imminent as was supposed.

A few days later Mrs. Judson was surprised by the return of Mr. and Mrs. Hough to the mission house. The belated ship upon which they had taken passage for Bengal was to be detained in port for some weeks, and their departure was deferred accordingly. Mrs. Judson hoped and prayed for the coming of her husband before they should go away again, that she might not be under the necessity, as she wrote, "of living in this dreadful country, and out here in the woods without a friend or protector."

Her daily program of study was resumed and diligently followed. "This," she wrote, "I find the best method to avoid dejection; besides, my conscience will not permit me to sit idly down and yield to those desponding feelings in which a Christian should not indulge."

Thus one day after another dragged by until a week spent itself in enforced study and anxious vigil. Each morning brought quickened hope and each night a fresh disappointment. But on one eventful day early in August, hope brightened into fulfilment and disappointment lost itself in a transport of joy. An English vessel had arrived at the mouth of the river, and — news almost too good to be true — Mr. Judson was on board! To his wife, the reaction from five long months of daily suspense was almost too much to endure.

In the living room of the mission house the husband and wife sat and recounted their experiences of the seven months of separation. Into her story of encouragement followed by disaster he could easily read the high courage and resourcefulness that had actually saved the mission from ruin. Into his narrative of fever, thirst, starvation, and disappointed hopes she read the high trust in God that had saved her husband from despair, if not from death. And together they faced the future, praying the old prayer of the first years in Rangoon: "God grant that we may live and die among the Burmans, though we never should do anything else than smooth the way for others."

Chapter 11

"THE EAST A-CALLIN'"

IN the year 1822 an English sailing vessel was making its slow passage between Calcutta and Liverpool by the old circuitous route around the Cape of Good Hope. On board were a number of European passengers returning home after a more or less prolonged stay in the East.

One of the larger cabins was occupied by three children and a sweet-faced lady evidently not their mother. The lady's brown eyes had a tired, patient look as if she had endured uncommon griefs, yet at the same time they shone with an unwonted fire as if proclaiming an experience fraught with high adventure. Her complexion bore that peculiar tan that seemed to indicate long residence in the tropics.

Her manner and appearance awakened something more than the curious interest of her fellow travelers, something strangely akin to reverence. During those days when she was prostrated in her berth, not by seasickness but by an old complaint, two young women of high social rank came frequently to inquire for her and to read aloud such portions of literature as she should select. Often her choice was from the Bible, to which she added her own clear-voiced entreaty for a life of self-denial and high service. Her two visitors were seriously impressed with the sincerity and purposefulness of this stranger who they discovered had been one of the pioneer missionaries to go from America to the Orient, and who, after ten years' absence, was on her way home for her first visit.

Yes, the traveler was no other than Ann Hasseltine Judson, who had bidden her husband good-by in Rangoon, Burma, and was now voyaging westward toward her girlhood home in America. Was there, do you think, no tinge of regret in her joyous anticipations of seeing father, mother, sisters, and all the dear, familiar scenes of New England? Leagues and leagues behind in old Rangoon lay the home of her womanhood, the first and only home of her married life. It had cost labor and sorrow abundant to establish that home, but the priceless treasure of one's heart is always won out of travail of spirit. Thus her life had become fibered deeply into the environment of heathen Burma, and to transplant it was like uprooting a firmly embedded tree.

"Rangoon, from having been the theater in which so much of the faithfulness, power, and mercy of God had been exhibited, from having been considered, for ten years past, as my home for life, and from a thousand interesting associations of ideas, had become the dearest spot on earth.

Hence you will imagine that no ordinary consideration could have induced my departure." These words Mrs. Judson wrote to a friend as she was leaving Burma.

It was indeed "no ordinary consideration," but a life and death concern that had compelled the long separation from her husband and her beloved work. She had become worn out by a deep-seated disease that foiled every attempt at its cure. Before his very eyes her husband had seen her wasting away, until the truth was forced upon him that unless his wife was sent at once to a more hardy, northern climate, she could live but a few months. It was a Spartan decision, but as Mrs. Judson said, "duty to God, to ourselves, to the board of missions, and to the perishing Burmans compelled us to adopt this course of procedure, though agonizing to all the natural feelings of our hearts."

Upon arrival in Calcutta in September, 1821, Mrs. Judson had found the captains of America-bound vessels unwilling to receive passengers, as cargoes had been accepted to the extent of their ships' capacity. Passage to England was therefore the alternative, and a kindly-disposed captain agreed to take her for a moderate sum provided she would share a stateroom with three children who were being sent to England. When the father heard of the proposition he offered to pay the entire cost of the cabin so that his children might have the benefit of Mrs. Judson's companionship.

Mr. Kipling has declared, "If you've 'eard the East a-callin', you won't never 'eed naught else." And so it was with Mrs. Judson. The farther she sailed toward the West the more tenaciously her thoughts clung to the Eastern city she had left behind. Before her eyes stretched the great expanse of ocean, but before her inner vision appeared a curiously wrought building, made partly of bamboo and thatch, and located on one of the pagoda roads in Rangoon. Memory and imagination haunted this place, for it was the scene of her most precious experiences of the last two years and was now the probable setting of her husband's daily labor. It was their wayside chapel, or *zayat*, as the Burmese called it, built by Mr. Judson on his return from the unfortunate Chittagong trip.

In the *zayat* Moung Nau had openly confessed his allegiance to Jesus Christ, esteeming it a rare privilege to be the first Christian convert among the Burmese people, even though he had naught to expect in this world but persecution and death. There, on the Sunday after Moung Nau's baptism, the Lord's Supper was for the first time administered by Mr. Judson in two languages, English and Burmese, an event that had been the desire of his heart for six long years.

In the open room at the front the learned teacher Moung Shwa-gnong had appeared day after day questioning and reasoning, his philosophic mind disturbed but not convinced until months later when he finally thrust aside fear of disgrace and persecution and besought Mr. Judson for baptism. In the inner room the Wednesday evening class was accustomed to meet with Mrs. Judson, and cherished were the memories of those evening hours.

Especially did her thoughts linger with her friend Mah

Men-la, that capable, influential Burmese woman, the first of her sex to acknowledge herself a Christian; who later, of her own accord, opened a village school that the boys and girls might not have to resort to the Buddhist priests for instruction. There was also her faithful sister Mah Myat-lah and there were Moung Thah-lah, Moung Byaa, and the rest of that stalwart little band of disciples, members of the church, twelve in number when Mrs. Judson left Burma. No wonder that she and her husband felt as if they had entered a little way into the experience of their Lord, whose heart was drawn out in yearning love toward his twelve disciples!

Never would Mrs. Judson forget the steadfastness of those first converts, three in number, who rallied around her husband in his hour of bitter discouragement, when he was on the verge of abandoning the mission and removing to Chittagong. "Stay," they said, "until a little church of ten is collected, and then if you must go we will not say nay. In that case we shall not be concerned. This religion will spread of itself. The Emperor cannot stop it."

It was the failure of the Ava trip that had wrought that depression of Mr. Judson's usually buoyant spirits. Oh, the chagrin and ignominy of that journey! Mrs. Judson's heart sank as she recalled the experiences that she had heard her husband narrate so often.

Mr. Judson, accompanied by his new missionary associate, Mr. Colman, had traveled in a native rowboat three hundred and fifty miles from Rangoon to the royal city Ava, that they might present to the Emperor a petition for religious freedom in Burma. Carefully they had prepared to conciliate his majesty with gifts, choosing as the most appropriate offering the Bible printed in six volumes, each volume bound in gold leaf and enclosed in a rich, embroidered covering.

And then Mrs. Judson pictured the missionaries' reception at the court of Ava, the splendor of the royal palace, vast and golden, and the proud, disdainful young monarch, with his rich, Oriental garb and gold-sheathed sword, and his commanding eye; before him the American teachers kneeling and humbly proffering their petition for freedom to preach Christ's gospel to the Burmese people!

It was a dramatic moment, a heathen emperor for the first time since the days of Rome confronted face to face by the quiet, determined followers of Jesus Christ! At first his majesty listened somewhat attentively and then reread the petition, handing it back without a word.

Breathlessly the two missionaries waited as he took the tract, beautifully printed for his benefit, from the hand of his minister of state, and read the first two sentences that assert there is but one eternal God, when, with supreme indifference, he flung it to the ground, thus deciding their fate. Two cutting sentences pronounced by the minister finally blasted their hopes: "In regard to the objects of your petition, his majesty gives no order. In regard to your sacred books, his majesty has no use for them; take them away." Then followed the ignominious retreat from the palace grounds and down the river to Rangoon to the solace of home and a few loyal friends.

One member of that little family group had traveled with Mrs. Judson from Burma to India, Emily Von Someren, who was returning to her childhood home in Madras to spend the time of her foster mother's absence. She could picture the child at ten years sitting sedately before a class of aged Burmese men and women teaching them their letters. And last summer Emily had been the mainstay of the household, when Mr. and Mrs. Judson were both sick with fever at the same time, with no attendant but the girl of thirteen. God had been good to lend them the little Dutch girl for so long a time.

Added to memories of the past came realities of the present, charged with pleasure unexpected. Soon after Mrs. Judson landed in England, Mr. Joseph Butterworth, an eminent Christian gentleman and member of Parliament, claimed her as the guest of his home. In his house she met many distinguished people, among them Wilberforce, Babington, and Somers, the King's chaplain. Afterwards Mr. Butterworth, in alluding to her visit, said that it reminded him of the apostolic injunction: "Be not forgetful to entertain strangers, for thereby some have entertained angels unawares."

Friends in Scotland heard of Mrs. Judson's arrival in England and urgently invited her to visit them, offering to defray her expenses. Thus she spent several weeks in that wonderful little country, with its thrilling history and stanch Christian people.

While there she received a letter from the Baptist mission board in America asking her to come at once to the United

States by the New York packet. She hastened to Liverpool
to take passage upon this ship, but was dissuaded by some
kind ladies in that city, who insisted upon paying her expenses upon a larger, more comfortable vessel.

Consequently, on August 16, on board the *Amity*, Mrs.
Judson recorded in her diary: "Should I be preserved
through the voyage, the next land I tread will be my own
native soil, ever loved America, the land of my birth. I cannot realize that I shall ever again find myself in my own dear
home at Bradford amid the scenes of my early youth, where
every spot is associated with some tender recollection.
But the constant idea that my husband is not a participator
of my joys will mar them all."

The beautiful coloring of October lay upon the New
England hills when Ann Hasseltine Judson returned along
the old Boston Road to her father's house in Bradford. The
voyage from Burma had hardly seemed so intolerably slow
as the last ten miles over which the stagecoach crept its
way.

One by one familiar landmarks came into view, well
remembered roads leading to neighboring towns, houses
where lived old acquaintances, a distant village on a hill,
and flowing swiftly through the valley, the dear old river
Merrimac. Excitement quickened every moment and was
at its topmost pitch when the cluster of white houses form-
ing the village of Bradford emerged in sight.

Now they are approaching Bradford Academy, the "pet
and pride of the community," yet still the same humble
little building in which Nancy Hasseltine and Harriet At-

wood went to school some eighteen years ago. And now at last they are drawing near the Hasseltine homestead and the welcome of father, mother, Rebecca, Mary, and Abigail.

What a home-coming it was! Ten years of absence and sometimes no letter from the wanderer for a year or more at a time! On her part, two solid years and a half of hungry expectancy before the first home letter arrived!

What wonder that the Hasseltine family felt almost as if they had received their youngest daughter from the dead! What wonder, too, that the house was thronged with visitors from morning until night, neighbors, friends, and kindred from near and far coming to welcome the girl they used to know, who, as a woman, had traveled farther than any of the stay-at-home New England folk had ever dreamed! And what thrilling, unimaginable experiences she had to narrate, and how the foreign missionary venture branded as "wild and romantic" ten years ago seemed to be justified in the light of the wonderful work begun in Burma!

It was a glad, proud moment for Miss Abigail Hasseltine, the preceptress of Bradford Academy, when her younger sister, always her favorite, stood before the academy students and told them of her loved work in the East, its hardships and hindrances and its glorious prospects. Like Miss Abigail, the boys and girls were captivated by the speaker's grace and beauty and thrilled by her wholehearted enthusiasm.

But, alas, Mrs. Judson had not counted the cost of this home-coming, had not once imagined its joy would exact so heavy a price. From the hour of arrival in her native land excitement robbed her nerves of their equilibrium. For the first four nights she was not able to close her eyes in sleep. Then came the immense shock of joy at the reunion with her family and friends, and for six weeks she could not obtain one quiet night of sleep.

The constant round of visitors, together with the cold of an approaching New England winter, undermined her health to such a degree that she was in a most alarming condition. The very purpose of her trip to America was being defeated, and however drastic the measure, she must devise some way to secure complete rest and quiet in a milder climate than Massachusetts.

One expedient suggested itself as feasible. Mr. Judson's only brother, Elnathan, was a surgeon of considerable skill working under government appointment in Baltimore. He had sensed the urgency of his sister's situation and had frequently written begging her to come south to take the treatment for her disease that could not be attempted with safety in the north. Her "Indian constitution," as she called it, was ill adapted to the rigors of a New England climate after long habituation to the tropics.

Thus, even in America, Mrs. Judson had to make heroic decisions, but heroic decisions seemed to have become almost the law of her life. It was a courageous act to tear herself away from her father's house after six weeks' presence and ten years' absence, yet it was her paramount duty to regain her health and to subordinate every other interest. So, late in November, she traveled bravely forth from Bradford to Providence, thence by steamboat to New York, where she paused for one interesting, memorable night.

A large number of people, hearing of her brief stay in the city, assembled to give her welcome and to pray with one accord for the mission work in Burma. It was a bracing experience to find such heartfelt interest in the faraway mission; yet the very exultation of feeling, mingled with thoughts of the distant home in Rangoon, wrought such a havoc of fatigue that she was scarcely able to proceed on her journey to Baltimore.

For the next four months Mrs. Judson made a brave struggle for health. Through her brother's influence she was attended by the most eminent physicians in Baltimore, who agreed in assuring her that she would recover by springtime but could not have lived through the winter had she stayed in New England. Even in the milder climate of Maryland it was no easy task to recuperate spent energy and heal the deep-seated disease.

Although for a time company was excluded and the coveted opportunity to tell of the need in Burma prohibited, yet even in her sick room Mrs. Judson worked daily for the mission she loved better than life itself. Many friends in England had besought her to write a history of the American mission in Burma of which she and her husband had been the founders. This she had essayed to do, beginning on shipboard during the voyage across the Atlantic, and now resuming the labor at the rate of five hours a day despite weakness and pain.

The book was written in the form of letters addressed to

Joseph Butterworth, Esq., M.P., London, her kind host and patron during her stay in England. Before Mrs. Judson left America her manuscript was printed, and today, in a few libraries and private collections, is still treasured the little old-fashioned volume in its original garb of 1823.

Of all the interesting mail from near and far that came to brighten Mrs. Judson's isolation, do you imagine anything brought such a thrill of satisfaction as those letters that bore the marks of long travel from Rangoon, Burma? One day in February a copy of Mr. Judson's journal reached his wife, and with breathless interest she read those closely-written pages. Five more converts to Christianity, among them three women who had formerly attended Mrs. Judson's Wednesday meetings in the *zayat!* Eighteen members of the church of Christ in Burma, a number pitifully small when you remember the millions of people, and yet hopefully large when you stop to think that from a heathen idol to a heavenly Father is a long way for the human mind to travel in its search for God! "You will readily imagine my anxiety to get back to Rangoon," wrote Mrs. Judson to her sister soon after the receipt of the Burmese letter.

When the opportunity for usefulness was so glowing with promise it was galling to one's ambition to be held captive in a sick room, yet in that period of quiet retirement from the world Mrs. Judson's spirit was being equipped for the great tribulation through which she was destined to pass. It seemed as if by her prayers she had entered into that shining region of peace and light where dwell the "very inhabitants of heaven," and had brought away something of its radiant atmosphere. God had become the solace and delight of her inner life, and from this time on "neither death, nor life, nor angels, . . . nor any other creature" would be able to separate her "from the love of God which is in Jesus Christ our Lord." This was just the armor her soul needed for its coming warfare.

In March and April Mrs. Judson spent several weeks in Washington, reading proof of her book, which was finished and in press. There, as everywhere she went, she left the impress of a lovely personality absolutely devoted to God and to the work he had given her to do in the world.

While she was in Washington, the Baptist General Convention, otherwise known as the mission board, held its annual session in the city. From its number a committee was appointed to confer with Mrs. Judson regarding the Burma mission, and at her suggestion several important measures were adopted. Those who came in touch with her on this occasion, as well as many others, realized as they had never done before the claim of Burma upon the Baptist churches of America, to whose efforts exclusively God had committed this portion of his needy world.

With the warmer weather of spring Mrs. Judson was able to return to Bradford, though only for a fleeting visit, because she purposed to sail for Burma early in the summer. In vain did her friends entreat her to remain another year so that her health might be completely restored. The voice of the East was "callin' " so audibly in her soul that she could literally " 'eed naught else." Some mysterious foreboding told her she was going away never to return, but this strange, solemn conviction no whit lessened her desire to depart.

On a June day in 1823, a large group of Christian people assembled at the Boston wharf to bid farewell to three missionaries who were sailing for the East, Mrs. Adoniram Judson and Mr. and Mrs. Jonathan Wade, destined, all three, for the American mission in Burma. The summer setting of this scene was quite unlike the bleak, wintry day in February, 1812, when the first missionaries from America to the heathen world sailed out of Salem harbor. As different, too, as summer is from winter was the expectancy singing in Mrs. Judson's heart, for she was this time on her way — *home.*

Chapter 12

THE GOLDEN CITY OF AVA

WITHIN sound of the pagoda bells in old Rangoon and within sight of the broad river leading to the sea, Adoniram Judson stood looking intently toward the west. His slight, alert figure and his keen brown eyes easily identified him with the young man who had led his classes and his classmates at Brown and Andover.

His face had always been that of the scholar, sensitive and thoughtful, but lines of invincible determination and marks of strong suffering now revealed his manhood's experience. Despite all the ravages of a tropical and uncivilized country for the last ten years, he was still youthful in face and form, still as immaculate in appearance, despite the old-fashioned cut of his clothes, as if he had just emerged from the tidy New England parsonage that was his boyhood home.

In point of fact he had just emerged from his well ordered

study in the mission house in Rangoon, the room that had been his perpetual retreat for the past ten months while he strove to banish anxiety and loneliness by unremitting application to study. During that period of waiting for his wife's return he had finished his translation of the New Testament and had written in Burmese a summary in twelve sections of the vast contents of Old Testament history, two enormous tasks, equal to the output of a dozen ordinary brains.

The stint of his mind was now accomplished, but the desire of his heart was not yet realized. When would the ship, bringing to him more precious cargo than all the costly merchandise that ever crossed the seas, come sailing into port? He strained his eyes seaward to catch the first glint of light on an approaching sail.

After Mrs. Judson had left Burma, more than two years before, her husband had again been enticed up the river to the royal city, Ava. His new missionary colleague, Dr. Price, had been summoned by order of the King himself, who had heard of the foreign doctor's skill and desired an exhibition of his ability. In this royal invitation Mr. Judson perceived an opportunity to press his claim a second time on behalf of religious liberty for the Burmese followers of Christ. On this occasion his hopes were not blighted as formerly, for the King and his court extended a gracious reception to the American doctor and teacher, and moreover displayed astonishing readiness to learn the meaning of the new religion that the Western strangers had introduced into the old Buddhist Empire.

After four months' stay in Ava, during which time he associated constantly with the royal family and government officials, Mr. Judson essayed to return home to Rangoon to watch for the coming of his wife. As he took leave of the King, his majesty protested against his going away and bade him come again and dwell permanently in the golden city.

A plot of ground had been given Mr. Judson as a site for a house, and his hopes ran high at the prospect of founding a Christian mission in the capital city of the nation. No tinge of foreboding darkened his thought as he retraced his course down the Irrawaddy to the port city of Rangoon.

It was early in February, 1823, when Mr. Judson returned home from Ava; it was ten months later, on the fifth day of December, when an English ship was reported at the mouth of the river and after some hours came sailing triumphantly into the broad harbor of Rangoon. The repressed longing of two years' separation breaks its bounds today, for, lo, the traveler has returned from her long, long journey!

It is verily Ann Hasseltine who has come back, not the Mrs. Judson who went away, frail and careworn, but the girl of olden days, with her fresh color, health, and beauty. What a traveler she has been, skirting the edge of four continents, compassing boundless leagues of ocean, circumnavigating hemispheres, and now safe and sound in the Burmese city from which she set forth two years and four months ago!

Yes, she has actually reached the home that lay always "at the end of her dream," but not, alas, to settle down in the mission house as hitherto, but to travel on, on to the chief city of the empire, where dwells the all-powerful, capricious King. Ava, the golden city, what is there in your simple name to suggest unbridled cruelty and despotism for all those who forfeit the favor of your haughty monarch?

Unwitting of danger, the husband and wife, accompanied by a few Burmese converts, set out for the new mission in the royal city. Mr. and Mrs. Hough, who had returned from Bengal during Mrs. Judson's absence, together with the newcomers, Mr. and Mrs. Wade, formed a force of workers sufficient to care for the mission in Rangoon. Mr. and Mrs. Judson, the intrepid pioneers, must press on to claim another heathen city for the one true God.

For six weeks in January and February, 1824, their little boat pushed its way against the wind upstream toward Ava. Often in the tortuous course of the river they walked through the wayside villages and overtook their snail-like conveyance. A foreign woman had never been seen in these inland towns, and great was the excitement when Mrs. Judson appeared. Friends and relatives were notified of her approach, that none might miss the extraordinary sight.

Within one hundred miles of Ava the travelers were confronted by a spectacle intended to strike wonder and terror into the hearts of beholders. The famous Burmese general, Bandoola, with his army, was making his pompous journey to the coast, confidently expecting to fight and conquer the armies of Britain.

His golden barge, surrounded by a fleet of golden war boats, met the humble little craft containing the missionaries and promptly challenged their right to proceed. When

informed that the travelers were not English people, but Americans going to Ava at the express command of the King, they permitted them to go on their way unmolested. From now on, however, the missionaries knew that war was a menacing probability and that at any moment they might be plunged into its grim realities.

A few days before they reached Ava, Dr. Price, who had heard of their approach, came in a small boat to meet them. It was a somewhat sorry tale he had to tell, dampening to their expectations of a welcome in the royal city. The tide of popularity had seemed to turn against the foreign residents of Ava. The old privy councilors of the King had been dismissed and their places filled by new officials who neither knew nor cared for the American teachers. Thus Mr. Judson foresaw that he had little to expect for the mission he and Dr. Price planned to establish.

When they arrived in the city, prospects were no less doleful. No house opened its door to receive them except Dr. Price's, which was unfinished and so unsavory with dampness that Mrs. Judson, after a few hours' stay, was thrown into a fever. There was no alternative but to abide in the boat until a shelter of some sort could be erected upon the plot of ground given by the King to Mr. Judson on his former visit. Mrs. Judson could hardly credit her senses when, in exactly two weeks after their arrival, they moved their belongings into a comfortable house of three rooms and a veranda, actually built and completed in that incredibly short time!

Therein, despite meager encouragement from the royal

palace, they began to hold services every evening, which a number of Burmese attended. It was a decided advantage to be able to speak the language with such ease as these two foreigners had acquired. Every Sunday Mr. Judson preached to an audience varying in number from twelve to twenty who assembled at Dr. Price's house across the river.

Mrs. Judson opened a school for girls, consisting originally of three small pupils, two of them being sisters whom their father had given to Mrs. Judson to educate. She named them for her own sisters, Mary and Abby Hasseltine, and planned to support one of them with the money that the "Judson Association of Bradford Academy" had agreed to contribute. In a spirit of quiet dependence upon God the missionaries applied themselves to their tasks, conscious, nevertheless, that trouble was brewing every day.

Mr. Judson went two or three times to the royal palace, according to his former habit, but the King scarcely deigned to notice him. The Queen, who had previously expressed a strong desire to see the teacher's wife in her foreign dress, now made no inquiries nor expressed a wish for her presence. Consequently Mrs. Judson did not attempt to visit the palace, although she was invited almost every day to call upon members of the royal family living outside the palace enclosure. The only course of procedure seemed to be to carry out their original intentions as unobtrusively as possible, seeking at every step to give evidence that they had nothing to do with the war.

Still, suspicion seemed to rest ominously upon the foreigners who dwelt at Ava. After the King and Queen took formal possession of the new palace just completed, an order was issued that, with one exception, no foreigner should be allowed to enter its precincts. This mysterious command was somewhat disconcerting, but for two or three weeks no alarming event occurred, and preparations were steadily made for the new brick house that was to shelter the Judson family from the blistering heat of the tropics.

On Sunday, the twenty-third of May, the little group of Christians gathered as usual for worship at Dr. Price's house, when, at the close of service, a messenger appeared at the door with an exciting announcement. *Rangoon had been captured by the British army!* War was a vivid reality now, and the foreigners in Ava must face its uncertain issues.

Mr. Gouger, a young English merchant residing in Ava, was in the company of the missionaries when the news arrived, and for his safety they feared more exceedingly than for their own. As Americans, they fervently hoped they would not be entangled in the affairs of war. Yet one and all repaired to the Judsons' house in the city to consult.

Mr. Gouger made haste to interview the prince who was the King's most influential brother. His reply was that his majesty had definitely stated that "the few foreigners residing in Ava had nothing to do with the war and should not be molested." Even with this assurance apprehension was not wholly allayed.

The cause of the war was that ill-fated country, ill-fated at least to the Judsons, known as Chittagong. This region was under British rule, and Burmese subjects often took refuge there from the despotism of their own government. The King of Burma demanded that his subjects should be arrested by British officers and returned to his authority. Furthermore, the Burmans resented the flag of Great Britain in a country which they felt belonged logically to their own nation.

Consequently, they made audacious advances into British territory and every attempt on the part of that government for redress was met by indifference, and finally by active preparations for war. So great was their daring that they even proposed to invade Bengal itself. It was rumored that Bandoola's army carried a pair of golden fetters to be worn by the Governor-general of India when he should be led captive to the "golden feet" of Burma's monarch.

In May, 1824, the British countered by sending to Rangoon an army of six thousand men under the command of Sir Archibald Campbell. So totally unexpected was this attack that little or no resistance was made and Rangoon fell promptly into the hands of the enemy.

When the news of the fall of Rangoon reached the royal city, almost gleeful preparations were made for speedy retaliation. Never a doubt was harbored of the possibility of victory, the King's only fear being that the British would be so overwhelmed with terror at the approach of the Burmese troops that they would flee away in their ships before they could be captured as slaves.

"Bring me," said the wife of a high official, "four white strangers to manage the affairs of my house, as I understand they are trusty servants."

In three or four days an army of ten thousand men was enlisted and sent on its way down the river toward Rangoon. As the war boats passed the Judsons' house on the river bank, the soldiers were dancing, singing, and gesticulating in high glee.

"Poor fellows," said those who knew the prowess of the empire that was at that time the greatest military power on earth, "you will probably never dance again."

As soon as the army had departed from the city, the government officials began to ask why the English soldiers had attacked Rangoon. There must be spies in the country who have invited them, was the insidious suggestion, instantaneously adopted. "And who so likely to be spies as the Englishmen residing in Ava?"

A rumor was circulated that Captain Laird, recently arrived, had brought papers from Bengal that stated the purpose of the English to take Rangoon. The three Englishmen, Mr. Gouger, Captain Laird, and Mr. Rogers, were summoned for examination, and were kept in confinement, though not in prison. Mr. and Mrs. Judson began to tremble for their own safety and were in daily dread of some direful event.

Soon the day came when Mr. Judson and Dr. Price were commanded to appear at the court of inquiry. Had they ever sent information to foreigners about the condition of affairs in Burma? They replied that they had always written to their friends in America, but that they had no correspondence whatsoever with British officers. After their examination was over they were not put in confinement as were the Englishmen, but were allowed to return to their homes.

Upon inspecting the accounts of Mr. Gouger, the Burmese officials came upon evidence that to their minds fully incriminated the American missionaries. As it was the custom of the Americans to receive their money by orders on Bengal, there were accordingly entries in Mr. Gouger's book recording payments of considerable sums to Dr. Price and Mr. Judson. Knowing nothing of such business methods, the Burmans concluded that the Americans were in the employ of the English and were therefore spies. The discovery was reported to the King, who, in angry tones, ordered the immediate arrest of the "two teachers."

On the eighth day of June Mr. and Mrs. Judson were quietly preparing for dinner, when suddenly the door was flung open and a Burmese officer rushed in, holding in his hand the dreaded black book, the sign of doom. Behind him pressed a dozen rough men, among them one whose spotted face marked him a jailer and executioner.

"Where is the teacher?" asked the officer's gruff voice.

Mr. Judson immediately came forward.

"You are called by the King," said the officer, in the form of speech used when arresting criminals.

As soon as the fateful sentence was pronounced, the spotted man seized Mr. Judson, threw him on the floor, and proceeded to bind him with the small cord used by the Burmans as an instrument of torture.

"Stay," cried Mrs. Judson, grasping the man's arm, "I will give you money."

"Take her, too," was the officer's brutal rejoinder. "She also is a foreigner."

With one beseeching look Mr. Judson entreated them to leave his wife until further orders should be received.

From that moment the scene was chaos personified. The neighbors gathered in frantic curiosity. The masons at work on the new brick house dropped their tools and ran. The little Burmese girls, Mary and Abby, screamed in terror. The Bengali servants stood petrified with horror at the insults heaped upon their master.

Meanwhile, the spotted-faced executioner, with a kind of fiendish delight, tightened the cords that bound his prisoner. Again Mrs. Judson implored him to take the money and loosen the ropes, but he only spurned her offer and dragged her husband away, to what fate she dared not imagine.

She gave the money to Moung Ing, one of the Rangoon Christians who had accompanied them to Ava, bidding him follow her husband and try to relieve his suffering. To her distress he came back with the report that when a few rods' distant from the house, the hardened wretches threw their prisoner to the ground and drew the cords still tighter, so that he could scarcely breathe. They marched him to the courthouse, related Moung Ing, where the Governor and city officials were assembled. There the King's order was read, consigning Mr. Judson to the death prison, that fatal place from which none ever emerged save by special intervention of the King.

From the courthouse to the prison enclosure Mr. Judson was dragged, and up the high steps to the one dark, filthy room where the hapless prisoners were confined. *Let-ma-yoon* was the name for this chamber of horrors, a name so hideously appropriate that those who knew the Burmese language shuddered at its mention. "Hand-shrink-not" was its meaning — shrink not from the most revolting cruelties ever devised by mortal man or incarnate fiend.

With the knowledge of her husband's committal to the death prison, that June day came to a close, leaving in Mrs. Judson's mind ghastly memories, but apprehensions yet more horrible. From that night began the extraordinary series of maneuvers for the rescue of her husband and the other foreign prisoners that made Ann Hasseltine Judson known in the East and West as the heroine of Ava.

Chapter *13*

THE HEROINE OF AVA

THE sunshine of a June afternoon in the tropics beat down upon the little house on the river bank in Ava where, on the fateful day of the arrest, Mrs. Judson was left alone with her Burmese companions. The first shock of terror was still upon her as she went into an inner room to face the horrible situation into which a few short hours had plunged her.

An unprotected foreign woman in the midst of an alien people whose every impulse was bent upon revenge! Her dearest companion in the world imprisoned and tortured, possibly doomed to death! The tragedy of her situation has scarcely been equaled in human history.

In overwhelming grief she cast herself upon the love and mercy of God, imploring strength to endure the sufferings that awaited her. Only infinite goodness could overcome the forces of cruel ignorance let loose in that heathen city.

Even the comfort of solitude was speedily denied, for the tramp of feet was heard on the veranda and a gruff voice demanded her appearance. It was the magistrate of the city calling the wife of the foreign prisoner to come forth for examination. Before obeying the summons she destroyed every letter, journal, and manuscript in her possession lest their existence should reveal the fact that they had correspondents in England and that they had recorded every happening since arrival in the country.

This task of precaution completed, Mrs. Judson presented herself before the Burmese official, who questioned her about every minute matter supposed to lie within her knowledge. This ordeal over, he ordered the gate closed, forbade any one to go in or out, and stationed a band of ruffians on guard, strictly charging them to keep their prisoner safe. With his duties thus pompously discharged the magistrate strode away.

The darkness of night fell upon the doomed house, and the gloom of death seemed to lurk in its shadows. Again Mrs. Judson took refuge in the inside room, drawing her little Burmese girls with her and barring the door behind them.

Instantly the guard commanded her to unfasten the door and come out, threatening, if she disobeyed, to break down the house. As persistently as they demanded, she refused, and tried to frighten them by declaring that she would complain of their conduct to higher authorities.

Finally, perceiving that she was determined not to yield, they seized the two Bengali servants and thrust them into

the stocks in most painful positions. Their plight was un-
bearable to behold, so Mrs. Judson called the head man to
the window and promised to give the guard each a present
in the morning if they would release her servants. After
loud argument and rough threatening, they agreed to the
bargain.

Their noisy carousings and diabolical language, combined
with the anxiety that pierced Mrs. Judson's mind like a
sword, made this June night a long-drawn horror. Sleep
was a faraway phantom and the darkness but a covert of
terror.

At the dawn of a new day Mrs. Judson's first move was
to dispatch Moung Ing to the prison to find out her husband's condition and to give him food, if he was still alive.
Moung Ing returned quickly with the news that Mr. Judson
and the other foreigners were confined in the death prison,
each bound with three pairs of iron fetters and fastened to a
long pole to prevent their moving.

The climax of agony for Mrs. Judson lay in the fact that
she was a prisoner herself and could make no efforts for their
release. Again and again she besought the magistrate for
permission to go to some member of the government and
state her case, but persistently he refused, declaring that
he dared not allow her to go lest she should make her escape.

Foiled in this attempt, she wrote a letter to one of the
King's sisters with whom she had been exceedingly friendly,
beseeching her to exert her influence on behalf of the foreign
prisoners. The note was returned with the message, "I do

not understand it," which in reality was a polite refusal to interfere. Afterwards Mrs. Judson learned that she had been really eager to help but dared not risk the Queen's disfavor.

The day dragged heavily past, and the darkness of another night settled down upon the little household of burdened people. To propitiate the guard, Mrs. Judson gave them tea and presents that softened their temper to such an extent that they refrained from molesting her throughout the night. Yet sleep came only in broken snatches, for perpetually before her mind loomed the vision of her husband, bound in iron fetters and stretched upon the prison floor.

When morning came Mrs. Judson arose, keyed for action. She had at last contrived a way to intercede for the prisoners. A message was sent to the governor of the city, requesting him to allow her to visit him with a present. This device worked like a charm, for immediately the guard received orders to allow their prisoner to go into the city.

The Governor welcomed his visitor graciously and inquired kindly what her desire might be. Whereupon Mrs. Judson related the situation of the foreigners, especially the two teachers, her husband and Dr. Price, who, as Americans, had nothing whatsoever to do with the war. The Governor answered that it was beyond his power to liberate them, but that he could make them more comfortable in prison. There was his head officer, he said, indicating an evil looking man; with him she must make terms.

The officer led her aside and tried to impress upon her the fact that he was complete master of the situation, and that the future comfort of herself as well as the prisoners depended upon the generosity of her presents to himself, which she must deliver secretly.

"What must I do," said Mrs. Judson, "to obtain a mitigation of the present sufferings of the two teachers?"

"Pay to me," said he, "two hundred *ticals* [about a hundred dollars], two pieces of fine cloth, and two pieces of handkerchiefs."

Mrs. Judson had taken a considerable sum of money with her when she left home in the morning, and this she offered to the greedy official, who, after some hesitation, accepted it and promised relief to the tortured prisoners.

Her next move was to request the Governor for a passport into the prison, which request was granted. But for the ghastly reality that awaited her there the most vivid imagination was scarcely prepared. In her own story of the unhappy days in Ava, Mrs. Judson refused to narrate the heartrending scene that took place that day at the prison entrance. Mr. Gouger, who hobbled to the wicket door at the same time, to receive his daily provisions, described many years later the pathetic meeting between the husband and wife.

Mr. Judson crawled to the door, as the heavy fetters around his ankles prevented his walking. The torture of mind and body that he had endured was stamped upon his face, which was as haggard as if death had already claimed him. His soiled, unkempt condition added to the misery of his appearance.

At sight of him, his wife buried her face in her hands,

unable to behold the shocking change that two days had wrought. Scarcely had they begun to talk together when the jailers ordered her away. She pleaded the Governor's permit, but they rejoined, "Depart, or we will pull you out."

Thus she was compelled to turn her weary steps away from the prison and walk the two miles back to her house, her mind freshly tortured by the prison scene, which was infinitely worse as a memory than as a conjecture.

That evening the missionaries, together with the other foreigners who had advanced an equal sum of money, were removed from the common prison and confined in an open shed within the prison yard. Here Mrs. Judson was allowed to send them food and mats upon which to sleep, but for several days entrance was denied her.

As her mind cast about for other expedients, she resolved to send a petition to the Queen herself. Mrs. Judson could not go in person to the royal palace, since no one in disgrace with the King was allowed admittance. Through the Queen's sister-in-law, who in better days had shown her marked favor, she would intercede with her royal highness.

Accordingly she chose a valuable gift and appeared in the presence of the Burmese noblewoman, who, as she entered, was reclining in Oriental fashion upon a carpet, surrounded by her attendants. Without waiting for the question "What do you want?" usually addressed to a suppliant, Mrs. Judson told of their unhappy plight and implored assistance.

Partly raising her head, the noblewoman examined the present and replied coldly, "Your case is not singular; all the foreigners are treated alike."

"But it is singular," said Mrs. Judson. "The teachers are Americans; they are ministers of religion, have nothing to do with war or politics, and came to Ava in obedience to the King's command. They have never done anything to deserve such treatment, and is it right they should be treated thus?"

"The King does as he pleases," she replied. "I am not the King; what can I do?"

"You can state their case to the Queen and obtain their release," answered Mrs. Judson. "Place yourself in my situation; were you in America, your husband innocent of crime, thrown into prison, in irons, and you a solitary, unprotected female, what would you do?"

With a slight show of feeling the woman replied, "I will present your petition; come again tomorrow."

This assurance sent Mrs. Judson homeward with the expectation, perhaps unwarranted, that the day of freedom was at hand.

On the morrow, however, her heart sank within her as she heard the news that Mr. Gouger's property, to the amount of fifty thousand rupees, had been seized and transferred to the palace. The officers, as they returned from the confiscation, informed Mrs. Judson that they should visit her house the next day.

It was a timely warning and she acted upon it by hiding away as much silver and as many precious possessions as she dared. As she thought of the danger involved in the act, her mind quivered with fear. If detected, her own imprisonment might be the penalty. On the other hand, the measure was imperative, since, if war should be protracted, there would be no way of procuring money, and starvation would be their doom.

True to their word, the officers appeared the following morning with an order from the King to seize the property of the missionaries. A lordly retinue seemed to be required to take away the possessions of a solitary foreign woman. The procession that approached the house was led by three Burmese noblemen, followed by a band of forty or fifty attendants.

The lady whom they had come to dispossess of all she owned received her visitors with marked courtesy, offering them chairs and treating them with tea and sweetmeats. They responded to her courtesy and to the high courage of her womanhood by conducting their disagreeable business with more kindliness than Mrs. Judson had ever expected to find in a Burmese official. Only the high dignitaries entered the house, the attendants being ordered to wait outside. Perceiving the grief that Mrs. Judson could not conceal, they even apologized for the necessity of their task, which they claimed was painful to them.

"Where are your silver, gold, and jewels?" inquired the royal treasurer.

"I have no gold or jewels," answered Mrs. Judson, "but here is the key of a trunk which contains the silver; do with it as you please."

The trunk was opened and the silver weighed.

"This money," interposed Mrs. Judson, "was collected in America by the disciples of Christ, and sent here for the purpose of building a *kyoung* (a priest's dwelling), and for our support while teaching the religion of Christ. Is it suitable that you should take it?"

The Burmese are habitually opposed to the acceptance of money given for religious purposes, hence the shrewdness of Mrs. Judson's appeal.

"We will state this circumstance to the King," replied an officer. "Perhaps he will restore it. But is this all the silver you have?"

"The house is in your possession," she said, evading a direct reply. "Search for yourselves."

"Have you not deposited silver with some person of your acquaintance?"

"My acquaintances are all in prison; with whom should I deposit silver?"

Examination of Mrs. Judson's trunk and dresser was the next command, and with some nicety of consideration they permitted only one of their number to attend her in this search. Everything that appealed to him as valuable or interesting was submitted to the other officials for decision as to whether it should be taken or left.

Mrs. Judson suggested the impropriety of taking partly worn clothing into the presence of the King, to which they agreed, and simply made a list of wearing apparel, doing the same with the books and medicine. Two particular treasures, a little work table and a rocking chair, were recovered from their grasp by a bit of stratagem on Mrs. Judson's part. Many other articles of unspeakable value to her during the months that followed were left behind when the work of confiscation was completed. Still, it was a ravaged, desolate home from which the officers and their staff departed that June day.

Scarcely had they disappeared down the road when Mrs. Judson hastened to the house of the Queen's sister-in-law to learn the result of yesterday's appeal. Loss of property was a mere bagatelle compared with her husband's imprisonment. To secure his release was a task that absorbed all her energies and fondest hopes, and, as time went on, exacted a superhuman patience. With hopefulness unrestrained, Mrs. Judson entered the presence of the Burmese noblewoman.

"I stated your case to the Queen," coolly announced her ladyship, "but her majesty replied, '*The teachers will not die; let them remain as they are.*' "

Mrs. Judson's spirits dropped like a meteor from the high region of expectancy into an abyss of disappointment. With tragic perception she knew that if the Queen refused to help, there was no one who would dare to intercede.

"Weary and heavy-laden" she turned away and retraced her homeward course by way of the prison, seeking the solace of a few minutes in her husband's company. At the prison gate she was gruffly denied admittance, and for ten days she was forbidden to enter, despite daily appeal.

The husband and wife then resorted to letter-writing, but after a few days the scheme was discovered and their messenger punished by beating and confinement in the stocks. They themselves were fined about ten dollars, besides suffering a torment of fear for the possible consequences of their daring.

On the morning following the seizure of her property Mrs. Judson visited the governor of the city, there to be met by a vigorous rebuke.

"You are very bad," said the Governor by way of greeting. "Why did you tell the royal treasurer that you had given me so much money?"

During the process of confiscation the officers had asked Mrs. Judson how much money she had paid the Governor and prison officers to secure the removal of the teachers from the inner prison. Naturally she had told the truth in reply, whereupon the officers went straightway to the Governor and extorted from him the sum stated. He became furiously angry and threatened to replace the teachers in their former condition inside the death prison.

To his accusation Mrs. Judson replied naïvely, "The treasurer inquired; what could I say?"

"Say that you had given nothing," retorted the Governor, "and I would have made the teachers comfortable in prison; but now I know not what will be their fate."

"But I cannot tell a falsehood," asserted Mrs. Judson. "My religion is different from yours; it forbids prevarication; and had you stood by me with your knife raised I could not have said what you suggest."

At this juncture the Governor's wife joined in the conversation. "Very true; what else could she have done? I like such straightforward conduct; you must not be angry with her." From that moment the Governor's wife became her steadfast friend.

At this welcome interruption, Mrs. Judson took opportunity to present to the offended magistrate a beautiful opera glass recently received from England, at the same time begging him not to vent his displeasure upon the innocent prisoners, promising to recompense him from time to time for the loss he had sustained on her account.

"You may intercede for your husband only; for your sake he shall remain where he is; but let the other prisoners take care of themselves."

Mrs. Judson pleaded earnestly for Dr. Price, but the Governor was immovable. That very day the doctor was returned to the dreadful prison filled with human victims, vermin, heat, and torture. After ten days he was again removed to the open shed, by virtue of a promised gift on his part and gifts received from Mrs. Judson.

From that time on Mrs. Johnson's life became a perpetual series of maneuvers to secure the favor of government officials on behalf of her husband. Hardly a day passed without a visit to some member of the royal family or government staff, when, with diplomacy unsurpassed in a woman, she pleaded the cause of the foreign prisoners.

To no avail were these daily visitations, save that frequent encouraging promises saved her from despair, and that, among those in high authority, many became her loyal friends who later aided with secret gifts of food and tried indirectly to create the impression in the royal palace that the Americans were in no degree responsible for the war. Yet no one had the courage to intercede with the King or Queen for repeal of the prison sentence so long as the British troops were continually defeating the armies of Burma.

Meanwhile, inside the prison enclosure, Mr. Judson and his companions suffered persecutions that the intrepid, resourceful wife could in no wise avert. Sometimes they were forbidden to speak to one another or to communicate with friends outside. Again they would be compelled to pay bribes for the delivery of their food or for the most trifling favors. At times the use of water was prohibited and fresh clothing denied them. Always three pairs of heavy fetters bound their ankles so closely that a shuffle of a few inches was the only possible step. Again and again they sought to close their eyes and ears when some fellow prisoner was tortured with the cord or iron mallet, or led forth at the fatal hour of three in the afternoon for execution.

Against this black background of horrors Mr. Judson's faith in God was like a shining star. Often he was heard repeating to himself the verses of Madame Guyon:

> No place I seek, but to fulfil,
> In life and death, Thy lovely will;
> No succor in my woes I want,
> Except what Thou art pleased to grant.

Many a time he expressed his belief that, following the war, conditions would be more favorable for missions: "It is possible that my life may be spared; if so, with what ardor and gratitude shall I pursue my work; and if not, his will be done; the door will be opened for others who will do the work better." Thus spoke another "ambassador in chains," with the same ring in his voice, the same thrill in his soul as was heard eighteen hundred years before in the Roman prison where Saint Paul was held in captivity.

Not satisfied with tormenting their immediate victims, the prison officials spent the remnant of their ill temper upon Mrs. Judson. For days in succession they forbade her to enter the prison until darkness fell, after which she would be compelled to walk two miles through the city streets to reach home.

"O, how many, many times," she wrote later to her brother-in-law, "have I returned from that dreary prison at nine o'clock at night, solitary and worn out with fatigue and anxiety, and thrown myself down in that same rocking chair which you and Deacon L. provided for me in Boston, and endeavored to invent some new scheme for the release of the prisoners. Sometimes, for a moment or two, my thoughts would glance toward America and my beloved friends there; but for nearly a year and a half, so entirely engrossed was every thought with present scenes and sufferings, that I seldom reflected on a single occurrence of my former life or recollected that I had a friend in existence out of Ava."

To Mrs. Judson the foreign prisoners owed everything that made prison life tolerable. Her husband was entirely dependent upon her for food and clothing, and often her resources were taxed to the utmost for a sufficient supply. For weeks at a time the only food she could procure was rice savored with *ngapee*, a preparation of fish, not altogether appetizing. One day she contrived a big surprise for her husband, and sent it by Moung Ing to the prison. It was actually a New England mince pie manufactured by much ingenuity out of buffalo beef and plantains!

The simple little act of devotion touched the imprisoned man to the quick. He had seen his wife standing like a queen at the prison gate; he had heard how she walked through the streets of Ava protected by an almost enchanted dignity, how her matchless courage won the hearts of jailers and nobles alike. He could almost thank God for trials that had caused the glory of her womanhood to shine with such luster. But this little touch of home was too much. He bowed his head upon his knees and the tears rolled down upon the iron fetters that bound his ankles.

Meanwhile the war was pushed with energy and determination, despite continual defeat. Bandoola alone had contrived to vanquish the British army, and, in recognition of his prowess, was recalled to Ava to be given command of the army sent to Rangoon. While in the city he was absolute master of affairs, honored beyond the King himself.

To this popular favorite Mrs. Judson resolved to appeal for the release of the imprisoned missionaries. Government officials warned her that it was a foolhardy act, but it was her last resort, and she could not forbear the attempt.

In secret Mr. Judson wrote a petition and one momentous day Mrs. Judson entered with fear and trembling into the presence of the proud general, who was surrounded by a crowd of flattering minions. One of his secretaries took the petition from her hand and read it aloud while Bandoola listened attentively, and at its finish spoke graciously to his suppliant, bidding her to come back again later for his answer.

In a few days she returned, taking with her a valuable

present. Bandoola was not at home to receive her, but he had left a message with his wife, which she modestly repeated to Mrs. Judson: he was now very busily employed in making preparations for Rangoon, but when he had retaken that place and expelled the British, he would return and release all the prisoners. An empty boast for Bandoola, and an empty hope for Mrs. Judson!

From that day she gave up the idea of escape from prison until the war should be ended. Yet she must continue those conciliatory visits to members of the government, lest the prisoners should forfeit the small measure of favor granted them. The governor of the city always gave her friendly welcome; in fact, set apart definite hours every other day when he counted on her coming to talk with him about American customs. He also permitted her to erect a little bamboo shelter in the prison yard where Mr. Judson could stay part of the time by himself and where she was sometimes allowed at her visits to spend two or three precious hours in his company.

Thus passed the days of that fateful year, one by one, until in January Mrs. Judson was seen no more in her usual haunts. Her husband, writhing in the fetters that kept him from going to her help, knew the cause of his wife's absence, which lengthened into weeks. He alone realized the loneliness and privation she was enduring in that uncivilized city, because, in the little house on the river bank, a baby child had come into the broken, suffering lives of its parents. Had it not been for God, who had never failed them even in their bitter affliction, Mr. Judson's agonizing

fear for his wife would have passed endurance. God's goodness would yet master this cruel oppression.

Twenty days after her birth the baby Maria was carried
to the prison to greet her father. Long before this time
Mrs. Judson had adopted the Burmese dress, believing
that the native costume would win the favor of the people.
There she stood at the prison door, her brown curls drawn
back from her forehead and fastened with a fragrant coco-
blossom, her richly colored gown, the gift of the Governor's
wife, clinging closely about her figure, which seemed to gain
height and stateliness from the costume designed for women
of smaller stature. In contrast to the Oriental hues of her
dress, her face was white and sad, but inexpressibly sweet.

In her arms lay the pale, blue-eyed baby, crying as hard
as if she understood the scene before her. Mr. Judson
crawled forth to meet them, and for the first time took his
child in his arms. Afterwards, during the long hours in the
prison, he composed some twenty-four stanzas addressed
to an "infant daughter, twenty days old, in the condemned
prison at Ava."

When Maria was two months old, her mother one day
received a frightful message from the prison. Mr. Judson
and all the foreigners had been cast into the inner prison
and bound with five pairs of fetters. His little bamboo
room had been torn down, and mat, pillow, and other
possessions seized by the jailers. The defeat of Bandoola
and the annihilation of his army, together with the advance
of the British forces toward Ava, had been the cause of
these vindictive measures against the foreign prisoners.

Mrs. Judson set forth at once for the Governor's house to see what could be done. The Governor was not at home, but, anticipating her visit, had left a message with his wife bidding her not to ask to have the extra fetters removed nor the prisoners released, *for it could not be done.*

From the Governor's house she went across to the prison gate but was forbidden to enter. The stillness of death hung over the prison yard. Not a white face was visible, and not a remnant of Mr. Judson's little shelter was left. Behind that closed door lay her husband in the filth and misery of the death prison, and here was she, only a few rods distant, but powerless to reach him or ease his suffering. There was naught to be done but return home and come again at an hour when the Governor was sure to be accessible.

In the evening she traversed again the two miles to the Governor's house, which was opposite the prison gate. As she entered the audience room the Governor looked up but did not speak, and his face expressed shame and pretended anger combined. Mrs. Judson opened the conversation.

"Your lordship has hitherto treated us with the kindness of a father. Our obligations to you are very great. We have looked to you for protection from oppression and cruelty. You have promised me particularly that you would stand by me to the last, and though you should receive an order from the King, you would not put Mr. Judson to death. What crime has he committed to deserve such additional punishment?"

At her words the old man began to cry like a child.

"I pity you, Tsa-yah-ga-dau (the name by which he always called Mrs. Judson). I knew how you would make me feel; I therefore forbade your application. But you must believe me when I say I do not wish to increase the sufferings of the prisoners. When I am ordered to execute them, the least that I can do is to put them out of sight. I will now tell you what I have never told you before, that three times I have received intimations from the Queen's brother to assassinate all the white prisoners privately, but I would not do it. And I now repeat it, though I execute all the others, I will never execute your husband. But I cannot release him from his present confinement and you must not ask it."

Never before had Mrs. Judson seen the Governor display so much feeling nor such firmness in denying her a favor. His words and manner aroused her worst forebodings for the future.

Meanwhile the scene within the death prison in Ava was not unlike the hell depicted by Dante and Milton, save that here there were a few brave spirits who "were still in heart and conscience free." The *Let-ma-yoon* was an old wooden building about forty feet long and thirty feet wide. It had no means of ventilation save crevices between the flimsy boards, no protection from the burning sun save the thin roof. Inside this one room were confined more than a hundred prisoners, men and women, most of them chained or fastened in the stocks.

The white prisoners were huddled in a corner, and a bamboo pole was thrust between the chains around their ankles, which at night was hoisted to an angle that left only the shoulders resting upon the ground. Occasionally Mrs. Judson was allowed to go to the prison door for five minutes, but mind and heart reeled at the sight of such misery. By dint of repeated appeals she won permission for the foreigners to eat their meals outside, but even this privilege was short-lived.

After more than a month in this vile place, Mr. Judson was taken sick with fever. His wife perceived that he could not live unless removed to more wholesome quarters. Consequently, that she might be near the prison and might the more frequently entreat the Governor for mercy, she moved from their house on the river bank to a one-room shelter that the Governor permitted her to build on his premises.

At last, worn out by her entreaties, he gave her an official order for Mr. Judson's removal and a permit for her to visit him at any hour to give medicines. Accordingly Mr. Judson exchanged the filthy prison for a little bamboo hovel so low that they could not stand upright, but, as Mrs. Judson said, "a palace compared with the place he had left."

Here, one morning after breakfast, Mrs. Judson was lingering with her husband, when suddenly a message was received from the Governor bidding her come to him at once. Somewhat alarmed by such unusual summons, she hastily obeyed. To her relief the Governor made only some idle queries about his watch and engaged her in affable conversation for some time. Unsuspectingly she took her leave and started in the direction of her room, when a servant came running toward her, his face pale with fright.

"The white prisoners have all been carried away," he gasped.

Scarcely believing so amazing a report, she hastened back to the Governor, who said he had just heard the news but was loath to tell her.

Distractedly she ran into the street, seeking to get a glimpse of the fugitives this way or that. But they were nowhere in sight. She darted down one street, then another, asking everyone she met, but no one would give her an answer.

At last an old woman declared that the prisoners had gone toward the little river on the way to Amarapoora. Mrs. Judson ran half a mile to the river bank, but no trace of the foreigners. Some friendly persons hurried to the place of execution, but lo, they were not there!

Again she resorted to the Governor for help, but he could only promise to dispatch a servant to discover their fate. "You can do nothing more for your husband," he said with slow emphasis. "*Take care of yourself.*"

With the Governor's warning ringing in her ears, she looked across to the desolate prison whose silent walls gave no answer to her restless question: Where, where are the foreign prisoners?

Chapter **14**

PRISONERS IN A HEATHEN VILLAGE

A BURMESE cart is at best a bungling contrivance for speed or comfort. Its wheels are simply round pieces of timber with holes in the center, through which a pole is passed to support the body of the conveyance. Springs and cushions are luxuries unknown. Through the sand and gravel of the hot season and the fathomless mud of the rainy season, the cart lurches and plunges at the uneven tread of the oxen.

One day in May, 1825, a cart of the usual variety bumped and thumped with the usual violence along the hot, dusty highway leading from Ava to Amarapoora. Under its shabby cover sat a motley group of travelers — two little Burmese girls, a Bengali servant, and an American woman with a baby in her arms. From Ava, in the early morning, the little party had set forth, conveyed for a few miles in a covered boat on the "little river," and then transferred to the stuffy, jolting cart for the remaining two miles.

At Amarapoora, their expected destination, a disappointment fell upon the band of travelers. The object of their journey was not yet attained, for lo, the prisoners who had yesterday been removed by stealth from the death prison at Ava were not to be found at Amarapoora. Only two hours before they had been sent on their way to a village four miles beyond.

Mrs. Judson, the leader of this little search party, or relief expedition, gave orders to proceed, but their cartman stolidly refused to go farther. Under the scorching sun of midday she bartered and cajoled for an hour, until another cartman agreed to convey them to Aungbinle, the miserable goal of their journey. Throughout that day of travel Mrs. Judson held the baby Maria in her arms, with no relaxation of tired muscles and nerves.

In the late afternoon, the village of Aungbinle was reached and the prison, the central place of interest, sought with haste. It was an old, tumble-down building in the last stages of dilapidation. Some workmen were on the top trying to manufacture a roof of leaves. While their abode was thus being prepared, the prisoners huddled together under a low projection outside, chained two and two and nearly dead with the immense discomfort of the journey.

There Mrs. Judson found her husband, a ghost of his former self, even his prison self. He gathered strength to say, "Why have you come? I hoped you would not follow, for you cannot live here."

Darkness was falling and Mrs. Judson had no shelter for the night. Might she put up a little bamboo house near the prison, she asked the jailer?

"No," he answered, "it is not customary."

Would he then find her a place where she might spend the night? He led her to his own house, which consisted of two small rooms, one of which he placed at her disposal.

It was a poor little place, half filled with grain and accumulated dirt, yet it harbored Mrs. Judson and her children not for one night only but for a long succession of nights and days. Some half-boiled water stayed her thirst and hunger that first night, when upon a mat spread over the grain she and her baby dropped in utter exhaustion.

In the morning she listened to the mournful tale her husband had to tell of the march of the prisoners from Ava to Aungbinle. Scarcely had she left the prison yard at Ava two days ago — so the story ran — when a jailer rushed in, seized Mr. Judson by the arm, stripped off his clothing, except shirt and pantaloons, tore off his fetters, tied a rope around his waist and dragged him to the courthouse, where he found the other foreign prisoners already assembled in a disconsolate group.

As soon as he arrived they were tied together two by two and the ropes given like reins into the hands of slaves who were to be their drivers. The *lamine-woon*, the officer in charge, mounted his horse and gave orders for the procession to start.

It was then eleven o'clock in the day, in the month of May, one of the hottest months of the year. Hats and shoes had been seized by the jailers, so there was no protection from the direct rays of the sun above nor the sun-baked earth beneath. They had proceeded about half a mile when Mr. Judson's feet became blistered and his fevered body so exhausted that, as they crossed the "little river," he would gladly have thrown himself into its cool waters and escaped his misery forever. But quickly he dispelled the thought as cowardice unworthy a Christian man. *They had still eight miles to travel!*

Before long the prisoners' bare feet became entirely destitute of skin. Every step was like treading upon burning coals, yet their brutal keepers goaded them on without mercy. When about half way they stopped for water, and Mr. Judson piteously begged the *lamine-woon* to allow him to ride his horse a mile or two as it seemed as if he could not take another step. A scathing, contemptuous look was the only reply he received.

He then asked Captain Laird, with whom he was tied, and who was a robust man, if he might lean upon his shoulder as he walked. Captain Laird consented, and so long as his strength lasted, supported his fellow traveler as they toiled along together.

Just as the limit of endurance was reached, a Bengali servant of Mr. Gouger's joined the ranks, and perceiving Mr. Judson's agony, tore off his Indian headdress made of cloth and gave half to his master and half to Mr. Judson. It was the work of a few seconds to wrap the cloth around the bruised feet and resume the march that must not be halted for sick or wounded prisoners.

The Bengali then walked by Mr. Judson's side and almost carried him the rest of the way. Had it not been for his timely help Mr. Judson would probably have met the fate of their Greek fellow prisoner who fell by the way, was beaten and dragged until his drivers were themselves weary, then carried in a cart to Amarapoora, where he died an hour after his arrival.

At Amarapoora the *lamine-woon* reluctantly decided to encamp for the night, realizing that his prisoners would perish on the way if forced to go on to Aungbinle that day. An old shed was secured for their resting-place, but what mockery of the word it was when none of the necessities were provided to ease their dreadful fatigue.

Moved by feminine curiosity, the wife of the *lamine-woon* came to look upon the foreign prisoners, and something more than curiosity stirred within her at the sight. She went away and ordered fruit, sugar, and tamarinds for their supper, and rice for their breakfast, which was the only food supply granted the famished men on their journey.

In the morning no member of the battered regiment was able to walk, and carts were furnished for their transfer to Aungbinle. As they neared the journey's end, they spent their small residue of strength surmising the fate that was to befall them.

Upon sight of the dilapidated prison they concluded with one accord that they were to be burned to death, just as the rumor circulated at Ava had predicted. They were endeavoring to fortify their souls for this awful doom when a band of workmen appeared and began repairing the prison. It was about this time that Mrs. Judson came to the end of her toilsome journey in the prison yard at Aungbinle.

Life in this uncivilized inland village marked a new stage in the suffering career of Mrs. Judson. It was now a fight for mere existence, for the bare necessities that hold body and soul together. The village boasted no market for food supplies and scarcely a roof to cover the homeless stranger. With her husband chained in the prison, her three-months-old baby dependent upon her for the very breath of life, two Burmese children clamoring for food and raiment, and a forlorn little heathen village as a background, PROBLEM would hardly spell Mrs. Judson's predicament.

The first of the new series of tragic adventures befell the Judson family the next day after their arrival in Aungbinle. Smallpox entered their household and fastened itself upon Mary Hasseltine, one of the Burmese girls whom they had adopted. Child though she was, Mary had been Mrs. Judson's only helper in the care of the baby Maria. Now the overtaxed mother must divide her time between the sick child at home and the sick husband in prison, who was still suffering from fever and his sorely-mangled feet.

From dawn to dark Mrs. Judson went from the house to the prison, from the prison to the house, back and forth, the baby borne always in her arms. Though she contracted a mild form of smallpox herself, she still continued her round of ministrations, serving not only her own family, but the entire community as well, since every child, young and old, who had never had smallpox was brought to her for vaccination! She had experimented upon the jailer's children with such success that her fame spread through the village. The foreign lady evidently possessed some charm whereby to ward off or lighten disease.

Gradually her patients recovered and the prisoners were established in more comfortable condition than in the death prison at Ava, being bound with one pair of fetters in lieu of three and five. But for Mrs. Judson the limit of physical endurance was reached. She had spent her strength for others' needs until there was none left to her credit and a miserable tropical disease took possession of her worn body. She became so weak that she could barely crawl to the prison. Yet in this pitiable condition she set forth in a Burmese cart to go to Ava in quest of medicines and food.

Upon reaching the deserted house on the river bank she was stricken with such a desperate attack that death seemed the only possible outcome, and to die near her husband's prison in Aungbinle was the one remaining desire in life. By taking small doses of laudanum at intervals she succeeded in quelling the disease to such an extent that, though unable to stand, she made the return journey by boat on the river and by cart through the mud to Aungbinle.

In sickness, home becomes the one charmed spot on earth, but what a home-coming was this! The end of the journey measured the end of endurance. The last vestige of strength vanished and her tremendous power of will was overthrown by the violence of the disease. The Bengali cook, who had been left in charge, came out to help his mistress, but at sight of her he burst into tears, so changed and emaciated had she become in the few days' absence. She stumbled into the little crowded room and dropped upon the mat, where she lay for two months, helpless with pain and weakness.

During Mrs. Judson's sickness the Bengali cook came valiantly to the rescue of the afflicted family. Day after day he provided and cooked the food, sometimes walking long distances for fuel and water, oftentimes delaying his own meal until nighttime that his patients' needs might be first supplied. He forgot caste and wages in his anxiety to serve the foreigners whom he loved. To this Hindu servant the Judson family owed the preservation of their lives during those weeks of dire want and misery.

Upon the youngest of their number fell the sharp edge of their misfortunes. Because of her mother's sickness the baby Maria was deprived of her natural food supply and no milk could be obtained in the village. Night after night the sick mother was compelled to listen to the wails of her child who was crying for food, and there was none to give! By sending presents to the jailers Mrs. Judson won permission for her husband to carry the baby through the village begging a few drops of nourishment from those Burmese mothers who had young children.

Afterwards, in narrating her experiences to the home people in America, Mrs. Judson wrote:

I now began to think the very afflictions of Job had come upon me. When in health, I could bear the various trials and vicissitudes through which I was called to pass. But to be confined with sickness and unable to assist those who were so dear to me, when in distress, was almost too much for me to bear, and had it not been for the consolations of religion, and an assured conviction that every additional trial was ordered by infinite love and mercy, I must have sunk under my accumulated sufferings.

To the stricken band of prisoners there came one day a faint gleam of hope. The *pakan-woon* had been convicted of high treason to the empire and promptly executed. Now this *pakan-woon* was the Burmese officer who boldly aspired to take Bandoola's place after his defeat and death. He made fair promises of large pay to the soldiers and guaranties of victory over the British army, so that the King was dazzled by his easygoing assurance and committed all power into his hands.

He was the bitter enemy of foreigners and it was during his high-handed reign that the foreign prisoners were removed from Ava to Aungbinle. They now learned for a certainty that he had sent them to the remote village for the express purpose of slaughtering them there and of coming himself to witness the gruesome spectacle. Frequently the news had spread through the prison of his expected arrival, but for what devilish intent no one had suspected. His death brought extension of life and hope to the war captives at Aungbinle.

It was not until six months had been lived out in the country prison and its environs that hope of escape definitely entered the Judson household. One day in November, 1825, a courier came to their door bearing a message from Mrs. Judson's loyal friend, the Governor, in Ava. Last night, so the letter read, an edict was issued in the royal palace for Mr. Judson's release from prison. The news was corroborated later in the day by an official order repealing the prison sentence.

With a joyful heart Mrs. Judson made preparations for departure in the early morning, when, lo, her plans were frustrated by the dastardly conduct of the jailers, who insisted that Mrs. Judson's name was not mentioned in the official document, therefore they could not permit her to leave the place.

"But I was not sent here as a prisoner," she protested. "You have no authority over me."

But no, she could not go, and the villagers should not be allowed to provide a cart for her conveyance. At this juncture Mr. Judson was removed from the prison to the jailers' house, where, by threats and persuasions added to gifts of provisions, they agreed to let Mrs. Judson depart with her husband.

It was noon the next day when the Judson family, accompanied by an official guard, left Aungbinle to return to Ava. At Amarapoora on the way Mr. Judson was detained for examination, and forwarded thence to the courthouse at Ava. With her little bodyguard of children Mrs. Judson pursued her own course and reached the house on the river bank at dusk.

In the morning she went in search of her husband and to her dismay found him again in prison, though not the death prison. She hastened to her old friend, the Governor, and besought an explanation. He informed her that Mr. Judson had been appointed interpreter for the Burman army in its negotiations with the British and that he was to go straightway to the army camp at Maloun.

Accordingly, on the morrow Mrs. Judson bade her husband farewell, while he embarked on the crude little river craft for the passage to Maloun. Upon arrival at camp, he was compelled to enter at once upon his task as interpreter, without so much as an hour to recuperate his lost energy. His stay in camp lasted six weeks and entailed sufferings equal to his prison experience, with the difference that chains were subtracted and hard work added.

Meantime Mrs. Judson drew a breath of relief, supposing that the value of her husband's services as interpreter would insure him kind treatment in the Burmese camp. Ignorance of his actual situation was a mercy, for there was no room in her life at this time for the added burden of anxiety.

Day by day her power of resistance grew less until she fell prey to that horrible disease, spotted fever. On the very day when she first recognized its fatal symptoms, a Burmese woman came to the door and volunteered her services as nurse for Maria. This incident was a direct expression of God's watchful care, because repeatedly she had sought to find a nurse for the baby and failed. Now in her exigency the help came without solicitation.

Once given entrance, the fever ran its course with violence. At the outset Mrs. Judson measured her weakness against its virulence and concluded it must be a losing fight. As the disease developed she tried to think how she could provide for little Maria in the event of her death and decided to commit her to the care of a Portuguese woman. As her mind was grappling with this painful question, reason failed, and trials and tribulations were swept into a whirl of delirium.

At this crucial moment Dr. Price was released from prison and hastened to her bedside. Had the doctor's coming been delayed a few hours she would probably have passed beyond human aid. In fact, the Burmese neighbors, in their childish curiosity, had already crowded into the house to look wonderingly upon the solemn spectacle of death.

"She is dead," they said in awe-stricken tones, "and if the king of angels should come in he could not save her."

Yet Dr. Price bent all his energies to the task of restoring the life that was being given in vicarious sacrifice for the Burmese people, though they did not know it. Vigorous measures were prescribed; her head was shaved and blisters applied to head and feet; the Bengali servant was ordered to press upon her the nourishment she had refused for days. As consciousness gradually returned, after days of delirium, her first realization was of this faithful servant standing by her bedside urging her to take a little wine and water.

By microscopic degrees, health, or its semblance, came again to the life shattered by anxiety, privation, and disease. One day during the slow convalescence, while she was still too weak to stand upon her feet, a message was brought to the sick room that left a panic of joy and fear in its train. Mr. Judson had been sent back to Ava and was under detention at the courthouse. What was to be his fate the messenger could not say!

During the night Mr. Judson had entered the city and had traversed the very street that passed his own door! A feeble little light glimmered within telling him the house was not unoccupied. But what unknown and fearful events might have taken place in those six weeks of absence! Oh, for one look behind that closed door!

He begged, bribed, cajoled, and threatened the jailers who constituted his guard, but to no avail. They pleaded the official command to deliver their prisoner without delay at the courthouse, which command they dared not disobey.

Consequently, Mr. Judson finished the night in an out-building near the courthouse, speculating anxiously as to his probable fate. On the river journey to Maloun he had chanced to see the official communication that accompanied him to Ava, "We have no further use for Yoodthan," the message read. "We therefore return him to the golden city." What new task would the "golden city" exact of its foreign captive before the price of liberty should be fully paid?

On the morrow Mr. Judson was summoned before the court session and hurriedly examined. Not one of his acquaintances was present at court that morning to identify him and explain the curt message forwarded from Maloun.

"From what place was he sent to Maloun?" inquired the presiding officer.

"From Aungbinle," was the reply.

"Let him then be returned thither," was the careless verdict.

The case was thus summarily disposed of, and the plaintiff dispatched to an out-of-the-way shed, serving as temporary prison, to await removal to Aungbinle. In these obscure quarters he spent a restless, tantalizing day. Here he was in the same city with his wife and child, separated only by a few minutes' distance, yet powerless to go to them or to hear one word of intelligence concerning them. Tantalus, parched with thirst and standing forever in the water he could not reach, was in no worse predicament.

Toward night Moung Ing came to his relief, having searched in vain for him throughout the day. At intervals this faithful Burmese had returned to the house to report his fruitless quest to the waiting wife. For her, too, the day had been almost insupportable. The "last straw" had been Moung Ing's discovery that her husband was ordered back to Aungbinle. She could scarcely breathe after the shock of these tidings.

If ever in her life Mrs. Judson felt the potency of prayer it was on that dreadful day. "I could not rise from my couch," she afterwards wrote. "I could make no efforts to secure my husband; I could only plead with that great and powerful Being who has said, 'Call upon me in the day of trouble, and I will hear, and thou shalt glorify me,' and who made me at this time feel so powerfully this promise that I became quite composed, feeling assured that my prayers would be answered."

It was in this desperate situation that Mrs. Judson resolved to appeal once again to the Governor, who had so many times befriended them.

"Entreat him," she instructed Moung Ing, "to make one

more effort for the release of Mr. Judson, and to prevent his being sent to the country prison," where, she thought wistfully, "I cannot follow and he must needs suffer much."

For the last time the friendly Governor came to the relief of the foreign lady who had so fully captured his homage. He sent a petition to the high court of the empire, offered himself as security for Mr. Judson, and won his release.

Early the next morning Mr. Judson was summoned to the Governor's house, there to receive the prize that is beyond rubies, his freedom. With a step more rapid, a heart more hopeful, than for two years past, he hurried through the streets of Ava to his own home.

The door of his house stood open as he approached, and, unobserved by any one, he entered. There, crouching in the ashes before a pan of coals sat a grimy, half-clothed Burmese woman, holding in her arms a puny, puny baby so covered with dirt that never for a moment did Mr. Judson dream it could be his own child.

He crossed the threshold into the next room, where, lying across the foot of the bed, as if she had fallen there, was the figure of a woman. Her face was white, her features drawn and sharp, and her whole form shrunken and emaciated. Her brown curls had been cut off and an old cotton cap covered her head.

Everything in the room spoke of neglect and ignorance in keeping with the face of the Burmese nurse who held the baby before the fire. In these squalid surroundings lay the beautiful, high-spirited woman who for fourteen years had never once "counted her life dear unto herself" if only she might follow the companion of her heart in his high path of service for God and man. "In journeyings often, in perils in the city, in perils in the wilderness, in perils in the sea, in perils among false brethren; in labor and travail, in watchings often, in hunger and thirst, in fastings often, in cold and nakedness; besides those things that are without" — daily anxiety for the little struggling Burmese church — thus ran the course of their Christlike sacrifice.

It may have been a tear that glanced her cheek, or a breath that came too near, or the sense of a dear, familiar presence more palpable than touch, for Ann Judson stirred uneasily in her sleep and opened her brown eyes — to look into her husband's face.

Chapter 15

THE BRITISH CAMP

U NDER the tropical moonlight that cast a shimmer
of gold upon the dark waters of the Irrawaddy, a wounded
British officer kept lonely vigil. He had been traitorously
attacked by the Burmese boatmen who manned his canoe,
robbed of his possessions, sorely injured in the fray, and
abandoned to his fate upon the deserted shore. For long,
restless hours he watched for the passage of a friendly craft
up or down stream.

As moonlight faded into daylight, a large rowboat, escorted by half a dozen golden boats, was seen approaching
from the direction of Ava. The wounded man waved a
signal of distress, which was instantly heeded by the passing
flotilla. A skiff was sent skimming over the water to his
rescue, and as if by magic he found himself on the deck
of a commodious rowboat, where the welcome accorded him
was more wondrous than magician's art.

Had thoughts of home woven a spell about his senses, or was he in solid reality looking into the face of a woman of his own race, the first white woman he had seen for more than a year in his military exile in Burma? She stood on the little deck leaning upon the arm of a worn, scholarly-looking man, evidently her husband. She herself was almost unearthly in her ethereal beauty, while her gentle speech fell upon his ear like a household hymn of his youth. His wounds were dressed and his head bandaged by a hand that had caught the art of deft and tender touch.

For two days, as the phalanx of boats glided slowly down the river toward the British camp, the wounded lieutenant discoursed with his new friends, reveling in the sense of home their companionship afforded him. In the daytime warmth and the cool of moonlight evenings they sat on deck recounting experiences novel, thrilling, and sad, that had been lived out in the heathen land of their exile.

Mrs. Judson sat in a large, swinging chair, in which her slight, graceful form seemed like a spirit scarcely touching this material world. At her feet lay the baby Maria, a poor little delicate baby, whose very frailty drew out the mother's fondest love. At her side sat her husband, watching with tender solicitude the play of her sensitive face as she talked. The British lieutenant, man of action that he was, listened spellbound to the vivid charm of her speech, made doubly eloquent in the presence of the tragic experiences of the last two years, revealing at once her sweetness of spirit and the alert vigor of her mind.

As the time came to part with the two persons who had

touched his life so briefly yet so indelibly, the army officer lingered wistfully, reluctant to pass out of their presence. As he looked for the last time into Mrs. Judson's face, while she was giving directions in Burmese to his new boatmen, tears gathered in his eyes, for with prophetic insight the British lieutenant foresaw that so delicate a spirit could not long remain in this human world.

For Mr. and Mrs. Judson the trip down the Irrawaddy in that month of March, 1826, was like a foretaste of heaven. Many years after the events recorded in these chapters, Adoniram Judson was in the midst of a group of persons who were discussing a moot question. What was the keenest pleasure ever experienced by mortal man since the world began? Some cited one instance, some another, revealing what men of different ages had regarded as supreme enjoyment.

Mr. Judson interposed. "Pooh," said he, "these men were not qualified to judge. I know of a much higher pleasure than that. What do you think of floating down the Irrawaddy on a cool, moonlight evening, with your wife by your side, and your baby in your arms, *free — all free?* But *you* cannot understand it, either; it needs a twenty-one months' qualification, and I can never regret my twenty-one months of misery when I recall that one delicious thrill. I think I have had a better appreciation of what heaven may be ever since."

Escape from Ava had been purchased on no easy terms for either foreigners or Burmans. In its childish egotism, the Burmese government had persistently declined all overtures for peace, imagining, like Mr. Micawber, that something would "turn up" to enable them to drive the British Army out of the country. But now that foreign army was actually advancing toward the capital city itself, and consternation was rife.

Two foreigners, Dr. Price and an English officer, were dispatched to the British camp to sue for peace, while within the nation's capital panic-stricken citizens built stockades and fortifications with furious energy. The house on the river bank where the Judsons once lived was torn down and the ground leveled for the placing of cannon.

Meantime the envoys returned and announced the treaty terms stipulated by Sir Archibald Campbell, commander-in-chief of the British Army. The Burmese government must pay the sum of ten million rupees, and must instantly surrender all foreign prisoners. The Judson family was specified by name in this latter order, upon hearing which the King exclaimed, "They are not English; they are my people, and shall not go."

For the past three months Mr. Judson's services as interpreter and counselor had become so indispensable to the Burmese government that consent to his departure would be reluctantly yielded. At that time both Mr. Judson and his wife were fully convinced that they would never be permitted to leave Ava.

As soon as peace terms were proclaimed in the royal palace, the Burmese officials began to haggle and shuffle, thinking that somehow the demands might be evaded, at the same time accusing the foreigners of double-dealing for

not securing milder terms. Again and again they procras-
tinated, thinking, in their ignorance of military principles,
that even though the money should be paid the British
Army would still continue its march upon Ava.

At last Sir Archibald Campbell issued an ultimatum: if
the sum demanded should be paid before he reached Ava,
peace would be concluded; if not, then war to the finish! All
foreign prisoners who chose to leave Ava must be released
at once, else peace would be forfeited.

Some Burmese officials remarked to Mr. Judson, "You
will not leave us; you shall become a great man if you will
remain." Adroitly he replied that his wife wished to go;
therefore he must follow.

At last the indemnity was paid, the prisoners released
from Aungbinle and sent either to their homes or down the
river to the British camp, and — *war was over!* On the banks
of the river Mr. and Mrs. Judson bade affectionate farewell
to the friendly Governor at whose house they had spent the
last two months, and left, as they supposed forever, the
"golden city" of Ava. Then came that blissful journey down
the Irrawaddy, the comradeship with the British officer whose
lot was cast with theirs for so brief a time, and finally, the
first sure token of civilized life — the outlines of an English
steamboat!

As their Burmese rowboat grated on the shore, two
British officers sprang on board to extend a welcome and to
proffer the hospitality of the anchored steamer. There Mrs.
Judson spent the remainder of the day, while her husband
went to the camp, a few miles downstream. In the evening

he returned with an invitation from the British general to come at once to his quarters.

The reception of a lady is always an event in army life, and she who was heralded as the heroine of Ava was to be the heroine also of the British soldiers. Unusual military honors were prepared for her welcome in camp. As a mark of especial attention, Sir Archibald Campbell sent his own son to escort her from the steamer.

Upon her arrival he himself stood on the shore to greet his guest and to conduct her to a tent more commodious than his own, boasting the uncommon luxury of a veranda. Through all his official courtesy ran the strain of a genuine fatherly kindness that would never be forgotten by its recipients.

The officers of his staff vied with one another in doing honor to their lady visitor whose gentle heroism impelled their deepest gallantry. Their courteous bearing contrasted as sharply with the gruff demeanor of the Burmese officers as civilization contrasts with heathendom.

"I presume to say," wrote Ann Judson in a home letter, "that no persons on earth were ever happier than we were during the fortnight we passed at the British camp. For several days this single idea wholly occupied my mind — that we were out of the power of the Burmese government and once more under the protection of the British. Our feelings continually dictated expressions like this: 'What shall we render to the Lord for all his benefits toward us?' "

An incident, half humorous, half pathetic, occurred a few days after the Judsons' arrival at camp. General Campbell proposed to give a dinner to the Burmese commissioners, and to make it an affair of pomp and magnificence fully expressing his nation's dignity. As if by an enchanted wand the camp was transformed into a wonderland of festivity, with floating banners and crimson and gold garnishings such as particularly delight Oriental fancy.

At the appointed hour the company assembled and, while the band played, marched in couples toward the table, led by Sir Archibald Campbell, who walked in solitary state. As the procession neared the tent with the veranda the music ceased, the grand march halted, and every guest, especially the Burmese to whom this scene was novelty personified, watched intently for the next act in the spectacle.

The general entered the tent and presently reappeared with a lady on his arm whom he led to the table and seated at his right hand. That was the psychological moment when the Burmese commissioners wished devoutly that the ground would open and swallow them, for that lady, honored above all others by the leading personage in the Burmese empire at that time, the general who had them completely at his mercy, that lady could place a black mark of condemnation against every Burmese official present, save one whose record was clean. She was the teacher's wife whom they had treated with incivility and cruelty in the day of her misfortune.

Judging by Burmese standards of ethics, their day of reckoning had come, for she would of course retaliate and demand their punishment. They and their wives would

seek revenge were the circumstances reversed. "Off with their heads" would be the military command next in order. Little they knew Mrs. Judson or the Christianity that inspired her life!

A glance around the table revealed to her the discomfiture of the Burmese guests. One poor man was suffering palpable remorse for his misdeeds. Perspiration covered his face, which was white and distorted with fear, while he trembled as if seized with an ague fit. There was sufficient reason for his qualms of conscience, for he was the culprit who had brutally scoffed at the misery he might have relieved.

One day Mrs. Judson had walked several miles to his house to beseech a favor for her husband, who was bound with five pairs of fetters in the inner prison and suffering from fever. It was early morning when she had left home, but she was kept waiting so long for an audience that it was high noon when she presented her petition, only to receive a gruff refusal.

As she turned to go, he caught sight of the silk umbrella she carried, and since it pleased his fancy he must needs possess it for his own. In vain she pleaded the danger of walking the long distance with no protection from the scorching midday sun. If he must have her parasol would he not furnish her with a paper one to shield her from the heat? Whereupon he laughed a sneering laugh, and replied that only stout people were in danger of sunstroke; the sun could not find such as she, thus mocking the very suffering that had wasted her to a shadow.

Mrs. Judson could almost smile now in recollection of the incident, especially at sight of the poor man's dismay, which pity bade her relieve. In her clear Burmese she spoke a few encouraging words to him, assuring him he had nothing whatsoever to fear. The British officers who had sensed the situation joined her in efforts to set him at ease, but with small success. Throughout the feast he was possessed by a fear he could not conceal. So much for the difference between Christian and heathen standards of conduct!

All too soon the time of departure drew near, when the Judsons must leave the friendly environment of the British camp and embark on the river journey to their old home in Rangoon. General Campbell arranged for their passage to the coast on a British gunboat, in which conveyance, more novel to the missionaries than a Burmese rowboat or Burmese cart, they returned to the city where, thirteen years ago, they had begun life as pioneers in the heathen land of Burma.

What had befallen the little church they had founded in labor and sorrow? Would they find it broken and scattered, or upstanding and stalwart? Had the eighteen Christian disciples remained loyal to their God through all the turmoil and affliction? A few hours would tell, for already they were in sight of the golden pagoda, the crowning landmark of Rangoon.

Chapter 16

THE HOPIA TREE

AFTER thirteen years of residence in Burma, Mr. and Mrs. Judson found themselves as homeless on their return to Rangoon in 1826 as upon that July day when they first landed in the forbidding country. The mission house had survived the ravage of war, but the mission itself had broken ranks and dispersed. The missionaries had narrowly escaped death and had fled to Calcutta to wait for the close of the war.

The Burmese Christians, eighteen in number, had scattered in alarm, though none but two had failed in loyalty to the holy faith they professed. Four of them hastened to Rangoon to welcome the Judsons, whose fate had been so long a sealed mystery to the world outside of Ava. In the loyalty of a common devotion to Christ they promised to follow the American teachers wherever they should go to build anew the shattered mission of Burma.

When Mr. and Mrs. Judson journeyed down the river from Ava to Rangoon they carried with them a trophy of priceless value. It was a little hard roll of paper that had been rescued, seemingly by miracle, from the death prison. To preserve the cherished possession from destruction, Mrs. Judson had artfully concealed it within the old pillow used by her husband in prison.

On that evil day when he was robbed of clothes and belongings and marched away to Aungbinle, a jailer seized the pillow, untied its covering, and flung away in contempt the meaningless roll he found inside. Some hours afterwards the faithful Moung Ing discovered the cotton-covered package and, prizing it as the only relic of the vanished prisoners, took it home and secreted it.

Many months later the hidden treasure was brought to light, and inside the tattered covering was found the unfinished manuscript of the Burmese Bible, upon which Mr. Judson had spent ten years of arduous labor. Surely it was God's hand that had saved those precious pages from destruction.

Eight years later the entire Bible was translated into Burmese. It has been said that Mr. Judson's Bible is to the Burmese people what Luther's is to the Germans and the King James version to English-speaking races. To the varied adventures of his missionary career, even in large measure to the tragic events at Ava, Mr. Judson owed his unique opportunity for mastering the intricacies of the difficult Burmese speech.

Ann and Adoniram Judson had been the pioneers of a

new civilization in Burma, but, like most pioneers, they had to leave the consummation of their labor for future generations to achieve and enjoy. As they walked through the squalid streets of Rangoon in March, 1826, the veil was not lifted from the future years to disclose the transformed structure that other workmen would build upon their foundations.

Since they were the first American teachers to arrive in Burma, they could scarcely discern, out of their small beginnings of Christian education, that there would some day be a Christian college named for them, and that in addition their denomination would establish Bible training schools, seminaries, and secondary schools with a total of thirty-eight thousand pupils. With only the simple hand press brought from Serampore to issue their modest publications, how could they foresee the well equipped printing establishment known until 1947 as the American Baptist Mission Press, that for many years would stand upon a thriving business street, employing two hundred men and women to print Bibles, schoolbooks, and other literature in the dialects of the principal tribes of Burma? When their little church could muster but three native members out of the desolation of war, how could such a diminutive band foreshadow the growth of their church, Lanmadaw, to its present active membership?

These beautiful realities of the future that would be achieved not only in Rangoon but in the chief cities and towns of Burma, were withheld from the eager gaze of the first missionaries. Their task was to "walk by faith, not by sight," and "blessed are they who have not seen, and yet have believed." The hope that inspired their pioneer labor was not unlike the Hope of Watts' picture, a baffled, blindfolded figure upon the "top of the world," drawing determined music from the lyre of one string.

To remain at Rangoon at the close of the war seemed a wholly imprudent course. Anarchy, famine, and wild beasts followed in quick succession. Tigers lurked in the outskirts of the city, carrying off cattle and human victims. Moreover the city was under British control for only a temporary period, pending the final ratification of peace terms, after which the old despotic régime would be resumed.

Thanks to the war it was no longer necessary to live under the Burmese government in order to live among Burmese people. Among the spoils of war Great Britain had claimed a long strip of Burmese territory bordering upon the seacoast. Already the region was well populated with Burmans, and refugees from the tyranny of Ava would throng increasingly within the boundaries of British justice. Somewhere within this borderland of humane government the missionaries would stake their claims for settlement.

As their thoughts were turning with the hardihood of the true pioneer toward the frontier country, Mr. Judson was opportunely invited to join the British Civil Commissioner on an exploration tour in the new province to determine the site of its capital city. In the very heart of the jungle the explorers decided to build the city of the future because the climate was invigorating and the elevation high and commanding. With a prayer of dedication, the British flag was hoisted and the infant settlement named Amherst, in honor of the Governor-general of India.

On the second day of July, 1826, the Judson family, preceded by the four Burmese Christians, removed from Rangoon to Amherst to create out of its wilderness a home and a mission. Even before they left Rangoon an old and unwelcome question had thrust in its claims for decision. The British Civil Commissioner was to be sent as envoy to Ava to negotiate a commercial treaty with the Burmese government, and Mr. Judson was urged to accompany him in the capacity of British ambassador. At first he vigorously demurred, having no relish for further encounter with the Burmese government and no heart to leave home after his long and painful absence.

Perhaps as bait for his acceptance, there was finally offered him that golden opportunity that he had never yet been able to resist. If he would join the embassy, they would agree to work for the insertion of a clause in the treaty insuring religious liberty to the subjects of Burma. A vision of the whole country open to the gospel of Christ broke down every scruple against the journey. With all her heart Mrs. Judson seconded the decision to go, regardless of the loneliness that she knew was in store for herself and Maria in their wilderness home.

In the little house at Amherst, vacated by the British Civil Superintendent for their occupancy, Mr. and Mrs. Judson prayed together and kissed each other good-by for the separation that promised to be far less long and hazardous than many they had experienced in their adventurous lives. They had been preserved through such extreme perils and hardships that an absence of three or four months, in circumstances of safety and comfort, seemed a matter of trivial import. In expectation of a speedy reunion and a home life sanctified by the sorrow of the past, Mrs. Judson watched her husband depart out of the peace of the tropical forest into the friction and discontent of the heathen city of Ava.

After he had gone she went eagerly to work, fashioning visible evidences of the mission they dreamed of establishing in the new Burma. Within the passage of two months' time, she had erected a bamboo house and two school-houses, in one of which she collected ten pupils for Moung Ing to instruct, reserving the other for the girls' school she planned to teach herself. Each Sunday she held services for the small but loyal congregation of Burmese Christians.

"After all our sufferings and afflictions," she wrote her husband, "I cannot but hope that God has mercy and a blessing in store for us. Let us strive to obtain it by our prayers and holy life."

When late September fell upon the unquiet city of Ava, Mr. Judson received another letter from his wife that rang with hopefulness and brought a tinge of relief to his constant solicitude for the little jungle home he had left behind.

I have this day moved into the new house [wrote Mrs. Judson] and for the first time since we were broken up at Ava feel myself at home. The house is large and convenient, and if you were here I should feel quite happy. The native population is increasing very fast, and things wear a favorable aspect. Moung Ing's school has commenced with ten scholars, and more are expected. Poor little Maria is still feeble. I sometimes hope she is getting better; then again she declines to her former weakness. When I ask her where Papa is, she always starts up and points toward the sea. The servants behave very well and I have no trouble about anything excepting you and Maria. Pray take care of yourself, particularly as regards the intermittent fever at Ava. May God preserve and bless you, and restore you in safety to your new and old home, is the prayer of your affectionate Ann.

The solace of this message brought to Mr. Judson no suggestion of the solemn, heartbreaking reality that a few weeks would disclose. No warning voice told him, as he chafed at the long absence from home, that away toward the coast in the frontier town of Amherst, the wife who had ministered to him with such matchless devotion would soon need his succor as she had never needed before and would never need again. How could he know that the slip of paper he held in his hand bore the last written word he would ever receive from Ann, his dearly loved Ann?

The annoying events of every day in the too familiar environment of Ava kept mind and heart busily occupied but perpetually disquieted. Associations too painful to recall, yet too evident to escape, preyed daily upon his senses. Again he was entangled in the maze of stupidity and conceit that comprised the government of Burma. And again, alas, he was confounded by the flat refusal of the King to grant religious freedom to his subjects. What unholy spell was cast upon the name of Ava to yield such a harvest of galling experience!

Why had he come? The trip had proved one long, unre-
lieved disappointment, yet at its outset it had looked so
promising, had seemed to indicate so plainly the path of
duty. With torturing insistence he asked that question on
the day in November when a black-sealed letter was laid
cautiously in his hands. Upon sight of the envelope, bearing
its emblem of grief, he concluded that frail little Maria had
lost hold of life. With thankfulness too deep for tears that
the mother was spared, he went into his room, broke the
seal, and read the opening sentence of a letter written by a
British officer in Amherst.

MY DEAR SIR:
To one who has suffered so much, and with such exemplary fortitude, there needs but little preface to tell a tale of distress. It
were cruel indeed to torture you with doubt and suspense. To sum
up the unhappy tidings in a few words, *Mrs. Judson is no more.* . . .

In broken snatches he got through the dreadful letter,
every phrase of which was written, as if by fire, upon his
heart. Early in October she was taken sick with fever so
violent that from the first a sure instinct told her she could
not recover. A skillful English physician was in constant at-
tendance, and through the kindness of the Civil Superintendent a European nurse was procured from the forty-
fifth regiment. Everything that a loving appreciation could
prompt was done for her comfort and healing, but to no
avail.

For two weeks the fever rose and fell, increased and
abated, until when its course was fully run, her strength was

also completely spent. On the sixth of October, in the dusk
of evening, her spirit went home to God.

We have buried her [so the letter ran] near the spot where she
first landed, and I have put up a small, rude fence around the
grave, to protect it from incautious intrusions. Your little girl,
Maria, is much better. Mrs. Wade has taken charge of her, and I
hope she will continue to thrive under her care.

Some weeks later, a brokenhearted man sat down in the
desolate house at Amherst and wrote to the mother of Ann,
over in the Hasseltine homestead in Bradford. This is the
story of those last days as his pen recorded it:

Amherst, February 4, 1827

Amid the desolation that death has made, I take up my pen
once more to address the mother of my beloved Ann. I am sitting
in the house she built, in the room where she breathed her last,
and at a window from which I see the hopia tree that stands at
the head of her grave, and the top of the "small, rude fence"
which they have put up "to protect it from incautious intrusion."
Mr. and Mrs. Wade are living in the house, having arrived here
about a month after Ann's death; and Mrs. Wade has taken
charge of my poor motherless Maria. I was unable to get any accounts of the child at Rangoon; and it was only on my arriving
here, the 24th ultimo, that I learned she was still alive. Mr. Wade
met me at the landingplace, and as I passed on to the house one
and another of the native Christians came out, and when they
saw me they began to weep. At length we reached the house, and
I almost expected to see my love coming out to meet me, as usual.
But no; I saw only in the arms of Mrs. Wade a poor little puny
child, who could not recognize her weeping father, and from
whose infant mind had long been erased all recollection of the
mother who had loved her so much.

She turned away from me in alarm, and I, obliged to seek
comfort elsewhere, found my way to the grave. But who ever ob-

tained comfort there? Thence I went to the house in which I left her, and looked at the spot where we last knelt in prayer and where we exchanged the parting kiss.

It seems that her head was much affected during her last days, and she said but little. She sometimes complained thus: "The teacher is long in coming; and the new missionaries are long in coming; I must die alone, and leave my little one; but as it is the will of God, I acquiesce in his will. I am not afraid of death, but I am afraid I shall not be able to bear these pains. Tell the teacher that the disease was most violent, and I could not write; tell him how I suffered and died; tell him all that you see; and take care of the house and things until he returns." When she was unable to notice anything else, she would still call the child to her, and charge the nurse to be kind to it, and indulge it in everything, until its father should return. The last day or two she lay almost senseless and motionless, on one side, her head reclining on her arm, her eyes closed; and at eight in the evening, with one exclamation of distress in the Burmese language, she ceased to breathe.

The doctor is decidedly of opinion that the fatal termination of the fever is not to be ascribed to the localities of the new settlement, but chiefly to the weakness of her constitution, occasioned by the severe privations and long-protracted sufferings she endured at Ava. O, with what meekness, and patience, and magnanimity and Christian fortitude she bore those sufferings! And can I wish they had been less? Can I sacrilegiously wish to rob her crown of a single gem? Much she saw and suffered of the evil of this evil world, and eminently was she qualified to relish and enjoy the pure and holy rest into which she has entered. True, she has been taken from a sphere in which she was singularly qualified, by her natural disposition, her winning manners, her devoted zeal, and her perfect acquaintance with the language, to be extensively serviceable to the cause of Christ; true, she has been torn from her husband's bleeding heart and from her darling babe; but infinite wisdom and love have presided, as ever, in this most afflicting dispensation. Faith decides that it is all right, and the decision of faith eternity will soon confirm.

In the spring of that sad New Year, the child Maria, aged two years and three months, was laid by the side of her mother under the hopia tree, which shaded their graves with its fair name of hope. Hope, sometimes blithesome and radiant, sometimes downcast and suffering, but always hope unconquerable, had inspired the life of Ann Hasseltine Judson from its beginning in the hill village of New England to its close in the jungle village of Burma. But lying deeper than hope, deeper even than faith, down in her heart of hearts was buried the secret that had transformed her life — "Whom, not having seen, I love."